"How Schools *Really* Work *is the best practical book on school improvement I have ever read. Saul Cooperman cuts through the mystery and the maze of education, and talks in concrete terms that everyone can immediately understand. His examples are clear and direct. If anyone is interested in making their school better, Dr. Cooperman tells them what to look for and what questions to ask.*

*"This step-by-step manual for local school improvement is a must for anyone who wants better schools. If everyone would act on Saul Cooperman's ideas, we would no longer need a nationwide school reform movement."*

**— Thomas H. Kean**
President, Drew University
Former Governor of New Jersey

*"No one in America knows more—or cares more deeply—about the functional implications of school improvement than Saul Cooperman. In* How Schools *Really* Work, *he shares his vast knowledge and commitment to school reform and renewal. This book is not only wise: it is eminently practical. Clearly written, full of lively example and illustration, it is as enjoyable to read as it is useful. Everyone who cares about school improvement should read this book, take its message to heart, and then act."*

**— David T. Kearns**
CEO, the New American Schools Development Corporation
Former CEO, Xerox Corporation

"How Schools *Really* Work *is a marvellous guide for parents, board members, administrators, and the community at large. It is written in language that anyone can understand. I only wish that I had had a copy of* How Schools *Really* Work *when I started to become involved in my children's education."*

**— Maude Dahme**
President, National Association of State Boards of Education

*"A plain English guide from a hands-on educator. Saul Cooperman knows America's schools. His book will help you know whether your school is right for your child."*

**— Lamar Alexander**
Former U.S. Secretary of Education
Governor of Tennessee

D1313206

*"Saul Cooperman has experience in all the critical positions in public education. His easy-to-follow, practical suggestions for lay citizens can also serve as a means of self-evaluation for those of us now serving in these positions. Cooperman's book can show educators what is essential for school improvement, the need for critical analysis, and the realization that educators should take the lead in change."*

**— Jill A. Eaton**
Principal, Walter Jackson Elementary School, Decatur, Alabama
Former President, Alabama Association of Elementary School Administrators
Former President, Southeastern Council of Elementary School Principals

*"Cooperman's experience, wisdom, conviction, and humanity radiate from every page. Parents and communities that follow his guidance will acquire the kinds of schools that America needs and in which their children will thrive."*

**— Chester E. Finn, Jr.**
Former Assistant Secretary of Education
Founding Partner and Director of Government Relations, The Edison Project
John M. Olin Fellow, Hudson Institute

*"One of America's leading educators, Saul Cooperman has written a wise, informed, and informative book. It is filled with insights that will be useful to both parents and educators. The book is based on his deep and wide experience. It is consistent with educational research on what makes schools and parents effective in bringing out the best among children."*

**— Herbert J. Walberg**
Research Professor of Education
University of Illinois at Chicago

*"I receive many letters from people who want to know how to make their schools better. How Schools Really Work tells them how, in useful, clear detail. While I have read several books trying to answer that question, this is the first, to my knowledge, to be written by someone who has held every possible position in the school system: teacher, principal, superintendent, commissioner of education.*
*"The thing I like best about this book is that it is so practical. It tells how education works, so that anyone can understand the problems and solutions, not just the symptoms."*

**— Joyce D. Brothers**
Psychologist and Syndicated Columnist

# HOW SCHOOLS REALLY WORK

# HOW SCHOOLS REALLY WORK

Practical Advice for Parents
from an Insider

# SAUL COOPERMAN

CATFEET
PRESS
CHICAGO

CATFEET

PRESS

Copyright © by Catfeet Press™

First printing 1996

Printed and bound in the United States of America

**Library of Congress Cataloging-in-Publication Data**

Cooperman. Saul.
   How schools really work : practical advice for parents from an insider / Saul Cooperman.
     p.  cm.
   Includes bibliographical references (p. ) and index.
   ISBN 0-8126-9335-3 (pbk. : alk. paper)
   1. School management and organization—United States.
  2. Education—Aims and objectives—United States.  3. Educational leadership—United States.  I. Title.
LB2805.0659  1996
371.2'00973—dc20
                                      96–41782
                                        CIP

*For Paulette*

# Contents

# Preface

**P**rincipal Charlie Henderson was just getting into his back-to-school night talk to parents: "Lincoln Middle School is one of the best in the state. I say this for many reasons; we have a choir that has achieved all-state status. We have introduced a new course in environmental education, which involves children with practical 'hands on' work in the community. We have introduced an English program that is extremely rigorous and ensures that each child in every grade will write a major term paper each year. Seventy percent of our teachers have masters' degrees, and over half of our teachers took at least one course at the University last year . . ."

As Principal Henderson continued to make his case most of the parents seemed to agree that Lincoln was indeed a fine school. But, during a ten-minute coffee brake, Andy Rizzo was talking with his wife Doris. "Honey, I'm not sure I agree with all that Mr. Henderson said. I think most of the teachers take courses so they can advance on the salary guide. And I don't think the courses teachers take have any relevance to what our children are studying, and besides I've seen some of the term papers that receive high marks and I think they are of low quality. I'm not buying all of Henderson's propaganda."

"Oh, Andy," replied Doris, "Casey is reading far ahead of her peers and Tim seems so happy with his train project. I don't know why you're so critical."

How do you know if your schools are working well? Are they failing or improving? How well do your school board and superintendent perform? What should principals do and are they doing it well? Do you have excellent teachers? Are they succeeding in their classrooms? Are they educating your kids?

This book gives you the answers to these questions. It tells you what to look for when you observe your school in operation.

Most school districts and individual schools insist that they are doing a good job, and indeed they may be. And, when criticism does come, schools, like most organizations, attempt to deflect that criticism.

They say, "It's not our fault." They complain that many parents don't take the time to work with their children. Parents, they add, do not set limits and children come to school with behavior problems. A diet of T.V. rather than reading for pleasure adds to the work of the schools. Furthermore, administrators and teachers point out that they are now responsible for feeding students—not only lunch but often breakfast as well—for instituting sex education programs, for monitoring possible child abuse, for teaching about the hazards of alcohol and drugs, and for providing before and after school programs for children whose parents are not at home.

There is a lot of truth in the 'not our fault' argument. But, should home and neighborhood situations, which often hinder the school's ability to do its job, be used to cover up shoddy performance within the school? Are these problems used as excuses for the school's inability to do its job? How can someone who wants to improve schools make the distinction?

Another way schools handle criticism is to say "Yes, there may be some problems; however, things are not nearly as bad as the critics want you to believe." At this point the school officials may switch the discussion to something they are most proud of, such as their extracurricular activities, the new counseling system in the junior high, or the 'gifted' program.

Is the school correct that the problems are minor and that there will soon be improvement? Are the other areas the school wants to focus on important? Should someone who wants the best schools pay as much attention to those areas as to the areas under criticism? How do you know?

Another defense often used against criticism is, "There are a few problems, but if people keep criticizing, the result will be lower morale and the staff will become defeatist." This approach attempts to lay guilt on the critic and reverses the tables by saying that the person who finds fault is the problem. It is called 'blame the messenger'.

Morale is important, of course, but facts must not be ignored. If children are not receiving a first-rate education, there is no excuse.

What is the situation in your school? Is there needless nitpicking and carping which affects the morale of people who are trying to do a good job? Or is the morale argument used to keep people away from the real problems that exist?

Another technique for deflecting criticism is to admit that there might be some problems, but to caution: "be careful not to move too quickly." This approach usually results in a committee of educators and parents being formed to study the issues, which often means that the really tough problems will not be discussed. Citizens and parents who see through this stratagem may be labeled 'politically motivated,' 'elitist,' or 'racist.' They know the established leadership will use 'committees' 'study', or 'research' to slow the pace so that the 'troublemakers' will lose heart and disappear. Yet, committees can get results. If the people on the committee are independent and tough-minded, if the objectives are carefully and specifically stated and the timelines tight, then good things can happen.

How does one make the distinction between responsible school officials who do not want to be rushed into premature solutions and those who establish tactics of a committee to give the appearance of action when they do not want to move?

How does one determine whether the school's reaction to criticism is responsible? The first step is to know whether the criticism has the ring of truth. This implies that we know what makes good schools. Do you know what good schools should look like? How do good schools work?

Schools are a people business. Over 75 percent of most school budgets are spent on the salaries and benefits of teachers, administrators, guidance counselors, secretaries, and custodians. Therefore, it makes sense to see if the people who comprise the school community are doing the things that will most benefit students. There is a world of difference between doing 'things' right and doing the right things. So the issue can be further narrowed to determining what are the right things to do.

I've chosen to examine schools through the key players: the teachers, principals, superintendents, and boards of education, because the ability to effect change at the policy level almost always involves all of them.

Some school districts and schools function well with all of the key players working as a team. There are bound to be disagreements, but everyone is doing the best he or she can for the children. The key players in other districts do not work well together. They spend more time on crass political maneuvers and self-serving behaviors. When things go wrong they seldom take responsibility for shortcomings, preferring to say "I'm working well, it's those other people who are at fault."

The school's performance depends on standards, behavioral and academic. If disciplinary rules are not clear and enforced, the school's progress will be minimal. If the school's expectations of its children are not high, there will be little progress in making education effective. If teachers, principals, superintendents, and school boards don't act consistently to uphold standards of conduct and scholastic attainment, then the schools will be limited to a tyranny of minimums.

Chapter 1 deals in turn with behavioral and academic aspects of discipline.

Chapters 2 through 5 look at the teachers, principals, superintendent, and school boards. I have focused on the most important aspects of each person's or group's performance. If your key players work well, your school district will improve its overall performance dramatically.

In the final chapter, I explain how to take on the educational establishment, and how to beat them, if that should prove necessary.

# Acknowledgments

I want to thank former Governor Thomas Kean, of New Jersey, for suggesting that I write this book; and Ray Chambers, for providing an atmosphere where I could get the job done. To each of them, wonderful leaders in different ways, I offer my most sincere gratitude.

To Blouke Carus and David Ramsay Steele, of Carus Publishing Company, my appreciation for bringing this book to publication. They made the process easy for a first-time author.

I sincerely thank Dan Jackson for his thoughtful reading of the manuscript and helpful criticisms. My gratitude is also extended to Lenore Greenberg, who offered timely comments.

# INTRODUCTION
# Why I Wrote This Book

**W**hen I showed a draft of this book to five outstanding public school administrators in my state, they said, "Saul, if you go ahead with this project, people will have the keys to our safe. Are you sure you want to upset the system by doing this?" I said that was exactly what I wanted to do. I told my colleagues that, for over thirty years, parents had said to me, "I want to improve our schools and I'm willing to spend time—tell me, Saul, how do I go about doing this? Where do I look? What do I ask?"

This book is my answer. The questions are the keys. They will allow you to probe deeply into your schools. Use this book as a practical manual to see how your teachers, principals, superintendent, and board of education measure up.

You will have the ability to ask the tough questions. You will see how areas connect with each other. With these keys you *will* be able to open the safe of the school establishment. If things are working well, treasure the teachers, principals, superintendent, and board of education. If things are not working well, you will not be manipulated.

No longer will you be confounded by schools or individuals who cover their ineptness with a smug "We'll be around after you move on." You will be able to make dramatic improvement for your children. And their *learning* is what it is all about.

# Who am I?

Perhaps you should know something about me. I am no politician. I have never run for office. I worked my way through the ranks of New Jersey's public schools as a teacher, vice-principal, principal, and super-intendent before being asked by a governor I did not know (but whom I soon grew to respect and admire) to become Commissioner of Education for a state with 88,000 teachers and 1 million students. I now head a non-profit company which works for educational improvement at all levels—national, state, and local.

In 1960, when I began teaching as a 25-year-old member of the social studies department at North Plainfield High School, I didn't often dream of where I'd be 35 years later. Like most young teachers, I spent my time learning the ropes and trying to keep from getting hit by the real or symbolic spitballs that are part of every educator's life in America.

With my wife, Paulette, I'd moved from the area near Newark, where I was born, and approached my first classroom job with great expectations. My three-year Navy experience completed the education I received earlier in the West Orange Public School system and at Lafayette College where I majored in Economics. As I needed to take a while getting my sea legs aboard the *U.S.S. Wisconsin,* I expected that getting used to the rise and fall of adolescent students would also take time. I was right.

During my first year teaching, I instructed approximately 140 teenagers. I unassumingly approached them with a sense of duty and commitment. In September, I vowed to favor none over the others and promised not to be distracted by the irregularities that sometimes seem to come up as a routine part of teenage life.

I was too young back then to envision my students' futures any more accurately than I could imagine my own. I may occasionally have mused about my future as a supervisor or principal and from time to time I would converse with children about their own plans for continued schooling. They shared dreams and hopes and aspirations. I tried to support their expectations in the way that most teachers do, while promoting the talents and honing the skills of various pupils.

But I soon began to sense that certain of my youngsters might fail. Tragically. Sadly. Predictably. And unnecessarily. During that first year of my career in education, I began to see how complicated my students' lives were. For the first time in my life, I saw clearly how good school experiences guided some of my kids toward future success while others were slowly doomed by factors that paved the way to failure in school and life. As I learned more and more about how teachers really operate and about how some administrators and boards of education function, the script for school mismanagement became clear to me in a private and professional way.

As I talked about my first students with Paulette, we both became concerned about their futures. Just as our hopes fueled dreams we shared for our children, we also hoped for the best in the lives of students I taught. But we also worried, as all new parents do, about how schools might fail to prepare these youngsters well for an American marketplace that was becoming more and more complicated.

With the little free time I had at that age, I also began thinking back to my own youth. While trying to find solid lessons for my students, I reviewed parts of my own childhood and found ways to connect my own growth as a person to the topics and themes we studied together in class.

# Bread and Butter Days

The Coopermans of West Orange were not so different from their neighbors. Like most Americans in the 1950s, we hoped to put the horror of mid-century war behind us. Our family looked forward to a peaceful stability that did not exist in the 1940s.

The Ambiellis and Shermans who lived on our block were good neighbors. We had a lot in common. The color of our skin and the size of our fathers' wallets didn't matter as much as how far you could throw a baseball or how long you could keep a yo-yo in motion.

With classmates our own age, my sister and I went to school year after year learning all we could about the values, heroes, and traditions of a nation that was coming into its own as a world leader. For me, the 1950s were exciting times when hopes and promises seemed real and reachable. Our teachers were men and women with vision, like my biology teacher Ed Eastwood. From them we learned to trust the future and value the past.

When I was a kid I liked reading about people who faced big problems squarely, especially those who dreamed about making things better than they were no matter how far they had to go to change things that were unfair. The 'Go for it' and 'Never say die' attitude of my heroes rubbed off one summer in a special way. My friends were all moaning and groaning about the fact that we didn't have a decent baseball field near us and had to go so far to play our favorite game. As we walked past this empty, overgrown four-acre spread that was unused, I got the brightest idea of my eleventh year.

"Let's build our own," I yelled.

My friends first thought that the idea was dumb. But as I started talking it up, they began to see the same possibility that I had in mind. We started by burning all the weeds and then clearing bags and bags of debris. Anyone watching us must have figured we were nuts. But after the first few hours of work, this crew knew what fast team effort could produce.

Within a relatively short time, we managed to clear the area and then raked out the infield surface needed for our baseball diamond. While the rest of the work was in progress, we went ahead and ordered shirts for the team we would soon become. In those days we liked the colorful uniforms of the Boston Braves. So we took the design of their outfits and had ours designed to look the same. I can still picture the tomahawk emblazoned across the fronts of our shirts. The pride we took in this entire do-it-yourself madcap undertaking stays with me now as one of the fondest memories I have of those days when no obstacle could hold us back.

There is another episode from that time which marked a major change in my life. I was shy. I rarely spoke directly to adults and never felt comfortable when called on in class to recite. I even backed away from relatives who routinely visited our house, actually retreating out onto the limb of a tree near my upstairs window for guaranteed privacy on weekend afternoons.

But all that changed suddenly one afternoon. The moment stays fixed in my memory like one of those delicious freeze-framed segments of a favorite movie. At this special instant I am standing on third base, representing our team's last hope for a tie scoring run during the final inning of a crucial late season game with our arch-rivals. Victory meant we'd go to the play offs. Defeat would mean having to wait until next year.

My team mate smashed a line drive that hit the bag at third and ricocheted into foul territory. I knew the rules that qualified this shot as a fair ball. The hit was legitimate. I deserved to score, so I raced home. Our batter was entitled to first and I remember yelling to him to leave the batter's box and start down the line. I crossed the plate triumphantly—since we'd at least tied—and turned to scream for our runner from second to follow me home with the go-ahead run. But our batter stopped half way to first because the ump called the shot "foul." Knowing the call was wrong, I pushed our batter toward first and believed the coach would set the record straight in the dispute after the bases were touched and the runs were properly recorded.

Ten seconds. That's all it took. My whole life that year hinged on winning this game and I knew in my heart and mind that the ump's call was wrong.

I kept yelling directions to teammates, forcing our batter to touch base at first, urging our runner from second to come on home anyhow with what would be recognized eventually as the winning run after the call was reversed. Pandemonium broke out. The ump's call confused everyone but me. I put my whole eleven-year-old heart into believing that the coaches would straighten things out *after* we had done what runners and batters have to do before officials get a chance to settle disputes over what's right and wrong.

Then injustice set in. The ump's call was not overturned! I was summarily sent back to third, our batter popped out to short, the inning ended, and our season went down the drain.

Not to be put off, I asked my father that night what could still correct the official blunder. He suggested I appeal to Miss MacMillan, our local school principal who acted as the well-intentioned but misinformed commissioner of baseball that year for our league. Miss MacMillan was a cross between Florence Nightingale and Lady Liberty, a beautiful administrator for an elementary school who had the wisdom of Solomon and the patience of a saint. I also understood that, when it came to baseball, she didn't know a balk from a bunt.

My audience in her office for the appeal was at 10:00 A.M. the following Monday. I went alone! I presented our case. I explained my disappointment, showed how wrong the call was, and pleaded for a reconsideration. I truly believed she might overrule the ump's decision, set the record straight, and restore some respect to our team's reputation.

No way. Miss MacMillan stoically explained that some things are just as they seem. Like my dad, she said there would always be some things in life that others wouldn't see as I did. She also cautioned me against demanding that people concur with my opinions on such disputed matters.

Disappointed, I left her office unsure of what to say or do. As frustrated as I was on that day, it occurred to me that I had fought my first real fight face to face with an authority figure outside my own family. Even if I lost, it gave me a sense of satisfaction that I had taken my teammates' cause to the top and debated an injustice done to us collectively by an ump less informed about the rules than I was at that young age.

In those days Duke Snider of the Brooklyn Dodgers was among the athletes I most admired. His boldness and grace filled my eyes with wonder when I watched him perform as daringly as he did. But in my early adolescence, the ball player I thought the most of was Jackie Robinson. In his style I found all the things any boy could cherish. His speed and agility made me imitate the way he'd slide into a stolen base. His calm under pressure made me dream of growing up to be the same kind of skilled performer. But what thrilled me most was his willingness to dare to change the racial status quo of America. I loved the way he so plainly put the lie to an old unfairness that had no legitimate place in the future of a country dedicated by its founders to the belief that all people are created equal.

My sports heroes were later replaced by college professors. At Lafayette College I flourished under the direction of many excellent instructors. But three stand out as irreplaceable parts of my personal development.

Outside of my major field of economics, Dr. Lewis Stableford managed to make biology a metaphor for life itself and I shall never forget how skillfully he brought my attention to the many possibilities of science from a philosophic or political point of view. He told me one day, sounding as historically certain as the Greek statue he resembled, that my skills were average but that my motivation raised my potential and promise above that of other students. From that moment on, I believed in myself as I never had before.

Morrison Handsaker and George Sause were Lafayette's best instructors in economics while I studied there. From the latter I learned to respect and value an insatiable interest in thoughtful planning and painstaking detail. But it was Professor Handsaker who took me to arbitration proceedings so I could watch him skillfully settle various disputes. These eyewitness opportunities, as no other lessons could have, gave me a chance to see how basic it is to be patient, flexible and realistic in all such endeavors.

As much as any of those sports heroes or teachers who influenced my way of seeing things, my dad should be listed in a place of high honor. Whatever other people meant to me during my development, none of them had as much impact on my world view as he did. His unexpected death shortly before my thirtieth birthday still fills me with a sadness I cannot explain in words. But no list of influences on my life would be complete without reference to his constancy, his strength, and the sense of fairness he instilled in me.

When I search now for one episode that tells much of what I learned from him, I recall a dispute in the neighborhood over the role of our rabbi. This man was from Poland and, unlike the American-born rabbis who were readily accepted, his pronunciation of certain words and his 'old world' ways seemed to make him unacceptable to part of the congregation. Despite the disapproval that would come his way, my dad championed the cause of this exiled teacher and finally gained community support for him. I remember Dad saying to me, "Here were Jews who were persecuted in America as well as other countries, turning on the rabbi. Not that he wasn't a good rabbi or a good person, but because he was different."

I was young when this occurred. It was not until years later that the full significance of my father's stance became precious to me. But after his death, I began to view this particular episode as his most genuine attempt to dispel unfairness. As many others whose dads were busy and successful, I took him and his health for granted. And like those whose parents are prematurely taken by a sudden, unexpected illness, I live with great regret over the abruptness of his departure. But when I think about him now, I know that he was all any boy could possibly want a parent to be. I admit without embarrassment that I still love and honor him as the greatest influence of my formative years.

## Up, Down, and All Around

Those were the men and memories that I spoke of most often in the first years of my teaching career. In some ways, I suppose, I tried to stay true to what they meant for me in my boyhood and pass on their significance to those I instructed. I taught and counseled boys and girls to know right from wrong. Often enough, like most teachers, I would pepper my lessons with bits and pieces of personal stories in order to show my youngsters how various subjects related to real life experiences. I also urged their parents to demand the most for and from their children, just as I did with the children my wife and I parented. Years later, after becoming an administrator, I insisted that those I supervised do the same.

But my own road toward that first teaching job was not a direct one. After I got out of the Navy I worked in sales in the Philadelphia area for a year. Our family was young. My wife and I spoke often about our future direction, but never for as long as we did on one special week-end in 1959. By the time Sunday night ended, we agreed I'd take the jump, leave business, and start teaching. The switch was not easy. It took a while to learn the ropes and it took even longer to master the subtle skills that distinguish good teachers from taskmasters. Like many other rookies, I sometimes felt the whole burden was on my per-formance. Then someone mentioned that it helps if adults do less so that a youngster can do more. That made a great deal of sense.

I like the story of the Martian who comes down to take a look at our schools. When he reports back to the head Martian, he explains that schools are essentially one big person doing a lot of work and a lot of little people watching.

As a new teacher I was a lot like that guy the Martian was talking about. I worked hard. I would come home every night exhausted. I was working, but my students weren't always learning. I remember in par-ticular the time I taught the unit how the United States gained control of the Panama Canal.

I lectured for a day on the chronological series of events and then spent two days questioning the students, making sure all of them responded several times. On the fourth day, I gave a quiz. I was pleased that the majority made either an A or B on the test. Obviously, I had communicated well and they had learned

About a month later I had reason to bring up the Panama Canal in the course of our class discussion. When I asked the students several questions, I saw a sea of blank faces. I was more than a little upset. It was only then that I learned the hard lesson of a freshman teacher. They were only learning what they thought I would ask on tests. The words and concepts were meaningless to them. The material was learned to be regurgitated, learned to be forgotten as soon as the test was completed.

The next year when I taught the same unit, I changed my strategy. I organized mini-units around "Why Nicaragua was a better place for a canal"; "Who needed a canal anyway?"; "Who was Philippe Buneau-Varilla and why should we care?"; "What was Colombia's role in all this?"

Each student had to read materials I had prepared on the mini-units and try to write their own sense of what happened. The results were amazing. Everybody was involved! At least half of the students came in to see me after school to discuss Nicaragua, Colombia, or the very interesting Mr. Buneau-Varilla.

When I referred to the Panama Canal later in the year almost all of the kids reacted instantly and correctly. I had discovered what educators today call guided learning. I organized and directed, but the students were involved and responsible for their work. What was 'dull' the year before became 'cool.'

# From the Frying Pan Into the Fire

As much as I loved the classroom in those early years, I was drawn toward administration by an urge to improve schools. Just as it took a while to learn the ins and outs of teaching methods, the lessons of a young administrator were also slow and painful. At times my brashness ran ahead of common sense and there is at least one episode that I recall now with a certain embarrassment. I do not regret having done what I did, but the story will show that diplomacy was not my strong suit.

Phi Delta Kappa is a well-known national educators' organization. Its members include some of the brightest of the bright and the savviest of educators. When my superintendent asked if he could nominate me for so prestigious a group, I was flattered and said "yes." At that time I had two choices as part of the Phi Delta Kappa admission procedures: to review and see if a dissertation study was applicable to the problems of the present, or to write an original paper that addressed a current problem. I chose the latter. I was concerned with the 'emergency certification' procedures. This meant that people could enter the teaching profession without meeting the requirements, because of teacher shortages. In short, standards were lowered because there was a demand for more teachers. I thought there was a better way: I thought we should change the system—raise standards; give qualifying examinations in the prospective teachers' academic major; overhaul the course work given in the universities; and finally, open the doors to talented college graduates who had not gone to teacher colleges.

That year there were 22 other young educators also nominated for membership in New Jersey. When the results came back, I was asked into the office of the man who had nominated me for inclusion into Phi Delta Kappa.

I found him seated at his desk with tears in his eyes. He sadly informed me that my candidacy was rejected and that Phi Delta Kappa would not accept so critical a paper as the one I had presented. I knew that he was hurt by my proposal to change the system and that my apparent dissatisfaction with academic routines disappointed him. But when all was said and done, I also knew that I had followed my heart and had written exactly what was on my mind. Even if my sponsor could not appreciate my intent, I felt justified in writing so directly. (This paper later became the basis for the 'Alternate Certification' program, introduced in New Jersey in 1983 and replicated in other states.)

Of course, it didn't help to learn that the other 21 candidates were all accepted and that my rejection was looked upon as some kind of unprecedented oddity. As glad as I was to have stuck to my guns, nothing, in the future that I envisioned for myself that day, seemed illustrious.

Over the next decade or so I acquired various administrative positions while gaining experiences wherever I went. In the course of twenty years, I got a chance to learn much about the levels of education because I worked in so many different capacities. After being a teacher, vice-principal, principal, and superintendent, I was honored to have my work as a commissioner recognized nationally and used as a model for reforms from coast to coast.

# And Now?

My mission is nearly the same as it was when I first entered teaching. Just as I was impatient with tired routines when I wrote that provocative paper for Phi Delta Kappa, I still become annoyed by those who resist improvement by lamely protesting "but we've always done it this way." If America has changed a lot because of the diverse and pluralistic shifts in our populations over the last twenty years, there still exists a gut need for us as people to stand by the hopes and dreams of the men and women who pioneered the way for us as a nation.

I see a chance for you as concerned readers to make decisions now that will alter the lives of youngsters to whom you are committed as I was devoted to the boys and girls I helped to teach many years ago. Yes, America has changed. Yes, its colorful variety continues to expand in dramatic ways, giving our country the diversity of a kaleidoscope. And yes, the problems facing an older generation now with the duty of educating today's students are greater than ever.

But that should not make us hesitate to dream of new answers to old questions. Our children deserve the best and they will be handicapped if we do not provide the kind of leadership needed to guide them into the 21st century.

Terrific teachers sometimes act a bit like cat burglars. Into their most memorable lessons they sneak special questions that act like the correct key from a ring with dozens of others. When they reach a youngster locked by the prejudices of an older generation, good teachers do a quick sidestep, skillfully reach for the right key, and untie students' minds by using the perfect question at just the right time.

I can think of many times when I was stopped in my tracks by a solid question from a virtuous journalist or by a student of mine asking for the truth or by one of my children at home unexpectedly inquiring about something that I would have thought beyond the child's age. How exciting it is to be faced with that kind of question, the sort that teases you almost like a riddle. That kind of question is like a key which unlocks the doors of the mind. It lets us in to areas that would go unexplored without it. The right inquiry, used at the moment when it's most needed, forces us to examine old areas of interest in a fresh way, thus opening our eyes to see future possibilities clearly for the first time.

The questions that are contained in my book will act as keys if used correctly. I'd like you to use these questions to unlock the secrets of your own school. If you get stuck entering the office of the principal or board member, all you'll have to do is flip back to the right section of this manual and refresh your memory before going on to get the results you want. Once you've learned how to use this book's strategies, you won't have to wonder how to question educators pointedly and fruitfully, for you will already have at your command the key questions that will enable you to get past the rusty locks that stop other outsiders. And once you've opened the right doors with the helpful guidance provided here, you will be able to show your children a clear path toward school success.

## Good Luck!

This manual can help you make quite a difference while challenging faulty assumptions and unproductive routines in schools, just as I tried to do in New Jersey. Lots of my former colleagues warned me against that. New friends along the way said my reforms tried too much too soon. They felt the teachers' union would be uncooperative or that parents wouldn't see that some changes were needed. Defense of the status quo would be the rule and I would be beating my head against a brick wall.

Although the warnings proved to be true, I continued to push hard because of my dissatisfaction with the 'we've always done it this way' attitude. Even if school employees knew there were better ways of doing things, most would forever embrace the existing routine, while mounting a public relations campaign to assure parents that their children were receiving a 'quality' education.

Meanwhile, students languished. The more I thought about their condition, the more upset I got. By the end of my first month as New Jersey Commissioner of Education, I knew I couldn't sit back and be a part of an oversized state machine run by adults who did not serve children as well as possible. I decided to change some things. We closely re-examined what kids learned. We made dramatic efforts to attract, develop, revitalize, and recognize teachers. We geared our efforts toward co-ordinating professional growth in direct relationship to how youngsters learned.

I will always remain proud of the men and women who worked with me to reform and improve the schools of New Jersey. The opposition we faced was difficult, but we made a determined effort to change policies for the better. And I do not now balk at giving concerned parents the kind of hardware needed to improve systems elsewhere while joining this school reform movement. These issues call for tough, roll-up-your-sleeves responses from men and women dedicated to making things better for kids. No one should be embarrassed while making a case in defense of their own children. No parents ought to hesitate about landing feet first on the desk of some administrator who's counting the months to retirement instead of keeping an eye on the future of American students.

Together we can continue a great tradition, begun by Ben Franklin and other founders of our nation, if we create new and better ways to educate. Use this book to get ahead of the game. While you're inching toward some slow success, don't lose either faith or hope. Remember that young minds and well-spent future lives are at stake here. When you're most tired and closest to quitting, start by saying the words of the most basic of all these questions: 'What's best for students?'

# 1
# How to Tell
# Whether Your
# School Upholds
# Standards

**D**avid Louis was reading an article in the weekly edition of the Center City *Eagle*.

> The reasons the schools don't have good discipline is because parents frequently raise their children without understanding two letters of the alphabet—'N' and 'O'. When the schools attempt to discipline children they are challenged by parents who are extremely permissive. . . .

"What bunk," said David, "always blaming the home for the school's shortcomings." "Personally," said his wife Carol, "I think there's a lot of truth in what the *Eagle* says. I was at a P.T.A. meeting, and when the principal talked about a student code of conduct that seemed eminently fair, a few parents went crazy. They said he had no right to impose such a repressive system on their kids. It sure seemed reasonable to me. How are principals and teachers going to get kids to learn if they can't hold them to reasonable standards of behavior?"

# Discipline

If we are to have a positive learning environment for our children, one which puts academic attainment first, then we must set a proper disciplinary tone in schools. And this means setting limits. Successful parents understand that the setting of limits is important to a child's growth. All children need love and encouragement, but they also need to know that discipline and the establishing of limits are necessary as well. Children understand that approval and boundaries are two sides of parental caring. And, it is during the time of greatest testing, during the teen years, that parents must be firm in the limits they want to establish. Most often the children who rebel also want to know what parental limits will be established.

Too often, of course, some parents and schools do not set limits and do not take the time to enforce the limits that they set. This does the children a tremendous disservice. It is interesting that when we have a great band director who demands spit and polish or a coach of a dominant basketball team who requires the students to get in shape and keep in shape, the students react in a positive way. We must set limits if our schools are to be safe and orderly. If this does not occur, very little academic education will take place.

A quick way to see if schools are safe and orderly is to **check the halls, the cafeteria, and the classrooms. Are the hallways clean? Do the people take pride in the fact that there are no scraps of paper on the floor or graffiti on the walls? Is the cafeteria cheerful and well-maintained? Is it monitored? Are scraps of food placed in the proper receptacles and not on the floor? The same goes for the classrooms—are they neat and clean? Do the teachers make them cheerful places, and do the students reflect the atmosphere the teachers are trying to convey?**

There are other factors you can use as litmus tests for how a school functions. **Are there assemblies in your schools?** Will the principals and teachers risk having 300, 400, or more junior high school students in one place at one time? If they do and the children are well-behaved, this tells you something very positive about the school. *If students seldom attend an assembly, you can be sure that the administrators and teachers don't have confidence that they can control the students.*

It would  be simple to understand this issue if we could tune in on the conversation of a fourteen-year-old and his parents after something had gone wrong in such a school during an assembly. Imagine the amused bewilderment of a father and mother during the following exchange.

"How was school?"

"Okay."

"Did you get tests back?"

"No."

"And lunch? Did you get to finish eating before you went to gym?"

"AAaaaaaaahhhhhhh . . . We didn't get to gym today."

"Really?"

"Really."

"Why not?"

"Why not?"

"Yes. Why didn't you get to gym today?"

Anyone who's seen teen movies or TV sitcoms about adolescent evasiveness will warm to the finale of this stereotypical parental exchange.

"Well . . ., we didn't get to gym today because we had an assembly earlier."

"Why would that have kept you from gym."

"Well . . ., things didn't go too hot at the assembly. As a matter of fact, after the vice principal stopped screaming at us, a few of the students were actually asked to go to his office for a while. Can you imagine that? Just for making a little noise at the beginning of the old assembly and then these boys wind up in all that trouble because they were just there in the wrong place at the wrong time . . . unfortunately . . . for them."

"Were you one of the boys sent to the office?"

"Me?"

"You."

"Believe it or not, I was."

"What happens next?"

"Mr. Snyder wants to see you in his office tomorrow and we may not have any more assemblies this year because it's hard to get everyone settled down to pay attention."

Now this sort of partial, self-serving explanation of disciplinary problems usually won't mislead a well-informed parent. Obviously, the episode is serious. Obviously, something is going to be done formally to rectify the situation and the youngsters involved are likely to receive severe but fair punishment.

But there is also a side to these matters that prompts many adults to smile knowingly (if only to themselves) while they think back to their own youth when similar wrongdoings were part of a half-understood rite of passage that sets childhood apart from the work-a-day world of adults.

So it seems hard for parents to know which kind of disruption a child's misbehavior represents. Is it the once-a-year mischief that even the best of youngsters occasionally resort to or is it the persistent nuisance that signals a deeper problem in a child willing to create behavioral difficulties in order to gain the attention of someone who might ultimately help?

If you think through the issue, what appears at home also appears in school on a larger scale. Everyone's children are sometimes messy. Everyone's kids are sometimes loud. And so on. Each home sets its own rules and tolerates a different degree of noise, impoliteness, or tardiness.

But a well-run school cannot afford to have such different standards. A consistent, reasonable, and publicized plan is called for when dealing with hundreds of children from various backgrounds. So the natural question that arises can be put this way. How does one establish a proper disciplinary level for a school? And how would residents of a particular district know if a decent and acceptable job was being done on this issue by educators?

*Begin by seeing if your school district and buildings have codes of conduct. The code must state exactly what is expected of all students within the school. Parents, administrators, and teachers must be involved in drawing up this code. What is written must be said in clear language. And most important, what is said must be enforced.*

The administration and teachers must keep at the task of discipline relentlessly. If teachers are doing their job in trying to maintain standards, then they must be backed by the administration and the board one hundred percent.

The test of the code of conduct usually comes in the form of the consistently disruptive student. Whatever should be done, whatever is appropriate, some students will challenge it. In almost every school, there are disruptive students. ***Does your school define what constitutes disruptive behavior? What plan does your school have for the disruptive student? Is that plan clear and known to everyone?*** If the student is disruptive, what chance does he have to receive an education?

I don't believe disruptive students should be tolerated. Students who have come to learn and teachers who want to teach should not have to put up with a disruptive student. Does our school have a carefully-delineated plan with regard to someone like this? Or ***is he like a ping-pong ball, going back and forth between the classroom teacher and the administrator? If 'ping-pong' is the approach, your school is failing the test of setting a proper level of discipline.***

Some schools deal with disruptive students by having a school-within-a-school, which usually has a program that meets basic curriculum needs and also has a heavy emphasis on counseling and interpersonal relationships. Other school districts have 'alternate schools' where disruptive students are told to go because they cannot remain within a normal school setting. Education is given in another building, distinct from the regular school. Some schools have programs where students attend classes for several hours a day. Then they are placed in work situations where they come into contact with positive role models. Still others provide counseling, if the students desire, and an opportunity to gain their diplomas by attending school from 4:00 until 7:00 P.M.

There are many approaches to alternate education for disruptive students. Certainly these students have a right to an education. Good school systems not only recognize this, but provide programs to help these students succeed. However, there must be a clear definition of disruption, and once a student falls within that definition, he or she must be removed from the regular classroom so that the other children can learn.

The consequences for a school without a clear code of conduct, or with one that isn't worth the paper it's written on, are serious. If a solid approach to discipline is lacking, then academic standards will slide, almost in direct relationship to the lack of discipline. For example, in an article for the *Wilson Quarterly,* Gary Sykes described the unspoken dishonesty of 'The Deal.'[1] "This occurs," says Sykes, "when there is no consistent code of conduct, when student expectations are vague or nonexistent, and when the administration does not stand behind the teacher. In situations such as this, teachers are frequently forced to make a deal." The teacher says to the student: "I know the administration is going to tolerate your behavior and I am going to have to keep you in my classroom for the rest of the year. I will not require much from you academically and I will pass you, but you must not upset the class and the other students who want to learn. If you won't act in a disruptive way, I won't ask much of you. We'll make a deal."

Result? The student is dreadfully shortchanged because he learns nothing. The teacher makes the deal because she simply wants to survive. She knows that she will not be helped by the administration and in order to keep her sanity and try to teach the other students, she bargains away academic integrity for the student's promise not to be disruptive. With several disruptive students in a classroom, the academic level is constantly pulled downward. The teacher must pay continued attention to the disruptive student who is not there to learn, rather than to the students who are.

Schools should have the right to establish limits with respect to dress. It's not particularly important that all schools within a county or a particular geographic area have similar policies. But what is important is that **students, teachers, administration, parents, and school boards discuss and then decide what proper attire ought to be.** For example, should hats be allowed in schools? Should all the boys' shirts be tucked in? Should shorts be allowed for both boys and girls when the weather is warm? Should shoes or sneakers be required? If tee shirts are allowed, should some standards be maintained with respect to what is written on them?

For example, which of the following slogans do you think a thirteen-year-old should be allowed to wear on a shirt at school?

a. Life's a bitch . . . then you die
b. Bon Jovi Sucks
c. Clinton Shifts like the wind
d. Underachiever and Proud Of It
e. None of the above

To sum up:

1. Disciplinary policies must be aimed at real problems.
2. All members of the school community must be involved in creating the disciplinary policy.
3. Misbehavior must be clearly defined and limits must be set.

4.  A clear and well-designed handbook to inform parents, students and teachers what the policy is, and what is expected of them, must be published.
5.  Disciplinary policy must be enforced consistently. Otherwise, the good words mean nothing.

How does your school measure up?

# Academic Rigor

"Julie, I see that Suzanne got an A on her report card in science. You can't do better than that!"

"But, what does that A mean?" asked Julie, "They spent most of their time observing how tadpoles become frogs. I know they had reading assignments and had to research some questions, but I still feel there should be more writing required."

"I don't agree," said Bob. "I think the school set some clear expectations; in fact I remember they asked us to check Suzanne's homework assignments and they sure were specific about the standard for that polliwog unit."

"You have some strong points Bob, but I think the overall academic rigor in science could be strengthened. They're doing an acceptable job, I guess. I just want them to be tougher academically."

Sometimes we forget that limits and standards hold just as true in academic areas as they do in areas of discipline. It is the primary responsibility of the school district to establish the standards and expectations with respect to academic rigor. These expectations start with the school board. Has your school board involved the community and professional staff to establish an overall policy toward academic results? Are these expectations set forth each year so that everyone knows what priorities are receiving the close focus and scrutiny of the board and the professional staff? In chapter 5, I will examine how a board of education sets a tone of academic excellence. It is of critical importance that overall academic goals be established, that priorities are clear and understandable to everyone and that the budget is linked to these priorities.

Excellent schools review their goals and priorities periodically. The community as well as teachers and administrators are involved in this goal setting and establishment of priorities. Good school districts and schools constantly discuss where they want to go and how they want to get there.

In excellent schools, goals and priorities are reflected in everything the school does. These goals come alive because the schools are committed to them. Teachers and principals are constantly asking the question, "Are the students learning what they are supposed to? Is the English Department meeting its goals? What can be done better?"

Good schools place the emphasis on learning and this takes precedence over all other school activities. Between the board of education and the faculty, there is agreement that any complex learning is going to depend on pupil mastery of basic skills. Therefore, there is constant attention to the progress of all students in the essentials of reading, writing, and math.

When this occurs students will quickly understand that the school exists to afford them an opportunity to learn. This attitude will surround them and will be pervasive. As frequently as they applaud athletes, public ceremonies will honor academic achievement. There will be a constant flow of information to students, parents, and the public with respect to the academic curriculum.

In elementary schools one should **check to see whether there are debate clubs, chess clubs, and science fairs. Are students involved in drama and are works of art prominently displayed in the school?** It is not unreasonable to expect elementary schools to encourage and recognize outstanding academic and artistic performance. Some middle, junior high, and high schools participate in academic leagues where they compete with each other in math, science, social studies, and foreign languages. I have attended several academic bowls within my state where teams from various schools research particular subjects and engage in a quiz show format. All of these activities say in one way or the other that academic achievement is important and will be recognized.

The use of time is precious when schools are concerned about student learning. Teachers do not talk about shortening the school day or working a shorter year. In states where mandatory collective bargaining negotiations exist, teachers do not talk about teacher-pupil contact time and try to negotiate fewer hours working with students. Indeed, the opposite is true. **In excellent schools, teachers seek the opportunity to work with students whether before school, during the regular school day, or after school.** Teachers are concerned with the notion of 'time on academic task', which means they pay attention to the amount of time students spend in learning. **Classes start on time** and the teacher makes sure that the student is engaged in the learning at hand. Everything is focused on learning!

Homework can have a real academic payoff, but homework must be carefully assigned and must stretch and engage the student's mind. It should not be assigned in a mechanical way or as punishment because the class misbehaved. Homework should require students to think, so they can apply what they have just learned to different situations. Homework can have a powerful effect on student learning, but it will be of little use if it is not corrected promptly. When it is not, the students know the teacher really doesn't care. Therefore, the students will conclude they don't have to do it or they can do it in a sloppy fashion.

Let me give you an example of what I am suggesting. Mr. Mitchell assigns a problem every night to his junior high school math class. To keep his students interested, he used topics which have meaning to teenagers. One day, "Mr. Mitchell's Problem of the Day" might be worded like this:

> The rock group 'Night Riders' was reviewing their revenues from their latest concert. They sold 20,000 tickets at $30, 1,500 T-shirts at $18.00 each, received 20% of the food sales of $23,000 and sold 600 tapes at $10 each.
>
> Costs to their agents were 10% of the total ticket sales, rent of the stadium was $50,000, publicity was $10,000 and local fees were 6% of the total revenues.
>
> What were the total revenues, total expenses and the net proceeds to the 'Night Riders?' If lead singer Carley Ringer got 50% of the net and the other four members of the group shared equally, how much did member Waldo Fimpert get?

Mr. Mitchell collects the homework first thing the next day and spends about five or ten minutes of class time discussing the problem. He corrects the homework that night and returns it to students the following day. He repeats this pattern every day. His students expect it and anticipate it. And because the problems are worded with their particular experiences in mind, they actually look forward to solving the 'Problem of the Day.'

- **Does your school district periodically review its goals and priorities? Are the community and faculty involved?**
- **Is there an emphasis on learning? Are basic skills stressed? Do teachers and administrators talk about extending the time students apply to learning or do they talk about less time for learning?**
- **Is there a policy on homework?**

# Expectations

The expectations that administrators and teachers have for students are extremely important. If teachers and principals believe that they can make a difference, they probably will. Excellent schools foster a 'can do' attitude; teachers and principals expect a lot from all students and take it as their responsibility to motivate their charges.

Educational literature has much to say about the effect of teacher and principal attitude on student learning. Wilbur Brookover has been a leader in determining what makes some schools effective. In Brookover's study *Schools Can Make a Difference* he found that "teachers and principals in high-achieving schools express the belief that students can master their academic work and expect them to do so. They are committed to seeing that their students learn to read, do mathematics, and other academic work."[2]

Michael Rutter, in an important book, *Fifteen Thousand Hours*, also found that staff attitude affected student learning. Rutter went on to say: "Adults and children seem to take school seriously in effective schools."[3]

When administrators and teachers believe that academic learning is at the central core of everything they do and that all students can learn, this attitude or ethos will permeate the whole school. When I focus more closely on teachers and principals in chapters 2 and 3, I will show that individuals whose expectations for learning are high will do certain things and be involved in activities which clearly help students to grow and learn.

The flip side of high expectations on the part of administrators and teachers is, of course, to lower student expectations. Teachers and administrators who 'give up' on their students are issuing a self-fulfilling prophecy. When this occurs, the remedy is new leadership that will do what must be done to enable children to learn.

This 'can't do' attitude is relatively easy to see and deal with. More troublesome is an attitude which appears 'realistic,' yet is detrimental to the student's future success. In two situations which follow, lowered expectations are the result of initially well-intentioned attitudes on the part of administrators and teachers.

These attitudes and expectations can often be seen in two phrases that are sometimes used in schools. The first, 'Don't blame the victim,' is directed toward the student who is the victim of his home and neighborhood. The second is 'Meeting the needs of students' and has as its central thought the attempt to find where the student is learning and to move the student from that point.

In the 'Don't blame the victim' approach, the student is seen as being disadvantaged by the environment outside the school. Pressure is often put on administrators and teachers 'to understand' the significant burdens and problems that children have. There is certainly much truth that many students come to school with significant problems and burdens. Parents may not be concerned on a day-to-day basis with the child's education. The student is more than likely from a single-parent family and often living at or below the poverty level. These pupils are often exposed to an enormous diet of sterile T.V. and when they venture outside their home, neighborhood role models are often the numbers' runners, fences, or drug dealers.

Educators point out that because of these home and neighborhood influences, students (the victims) will be ill-equipped to handle schoolwork. If challenged with conflicting values, they may become hostile and get out of control. Attempts at discipline will deteriorate into chaotic situations.

I had a recent conversation with a young teacher who works with youngsters in Newark, New Jersey. He comes well-equipped to handle his new responsibilities as a teacher in one of New Jersey's largest urban settings. But in the course of our conversation, I got the impression he was more distracted by grim headlines and doomsday prophesying than by the actual realities that he faced in the first months of his chosen vocation.

"Do you know," he asked rhetorically, "that over a million teens get pregnant each year?"

I said I was aware of the discouraging statistics and supported school efforts to do something about the part of that problem that can be helped by educators.

"Do you realize that three million teenagers contract sexually transmitted diseases each year? That makes adolescents the highest risk group of any segment of the population and nearly 25 percent of those who are sexually active will be infected."

I replied that I was aware of statistics like these, but added that some experts are relieved by the fact that so many youngsters now come for help sooner than their counterparts in earlier decades.

"Well," he continued, "the typical student in adolescence today has tried marijuana and many use it regularly."

"No. I think that the typical student has not done that. Some surveys do place the number in the two to three million range for all the millions of students between 12 and 17 years of age. But that doesn't mean that it's typical, because the vast majority of kids have not tried marijuana and they know its harmful effects."

"But the statistics are alarming. You have to look at the numbers when you try to imagine how hard it is to raise children today," he said.

"Well," I responded, "the numbers do frighten some observers and they discourage others from trying to help as you are by rolling up your sleeves and teaching the best you can under circumstances that make things hard."

There is no doubt that many students come to school with heavy burdens. They have not had the advantages of a strong family situation where limits are established and character formation is important. In many ways, they are the victims of a world they didn't create.

However, administrators and teachers should understand that to the degree that sensitivity and empathy are rationalized into thinking that we can't expect much, then schools set their sights much too low. This insidious belief that schools cannot help students learn creates lethargic people and school systems which hide behind real problems to cover their own inept performance and lack of commitment. 'What can I do?' is their lament. Instead of following the lead of districts and schools who light the candles of student success, they continue to curse the darkness.

Some teachers and administrators who recognize the very real aspects of the so-called victims' background try to find a middle ground. They want improvement, but recognize they must begin where the student is, academically and socially. This is often verbalized in the statement: "I'm trying to meet their needs."

# 'Meeting Needs'

This type of statement seems sensitive and caring. Schools should not push students so they are in over their heads, frustrated by artificially high standards and doomed to failure. Yet on the other hand, 'meeting the needs of my students' often means *a lowering of standards and expectations to what the student puts forth and then simply moving the student ahead grade after grade.* As students perform less ably, the course content is 'adjusted'; standards are lowered so that the student can 'achieve' and move on through the graded structure. At the same time grades are raised to make sure that the advancement is continuous. Schools have diminished the curriculum and pushed the student ahead on the easiest possible path. All this happens under the rubric of 'meeting the needs of my students.'

One of the factors that often brings diminishing academic standards and lowered expectations in some schools is the fear of dropouts. Administrators and teachers don't want such numbers to increase because they will reflect negatively on their performance. So standards are lowered to keep students in school. Students may learn little, but the dropout numbers look better.

You can infer how often a false concern over those dropout numbers informs school policy from what's said between the lines of this conversation between two guidance counselors.

"So are we going to start having that General Math class for the kids who can't pass Algebra?"

"Looks that way. We certainly have the numbers to justify it."

"And it'll be practical for them, I hope!"

"Well . . ., I wouldn't count on it doing wonders for our SAT scores, if you know what I mean."

"Quit joking. I know they're not bright kids. And some may even quit school no matter what we try. But will the class have a solid practical basis in day-to-day math needs? And who's teaching it?"

"Whoa, boy! It's just a general math class. We don't get Einstein to teach it and we don't turn the kids into future mathematicians and accountants, so don't expect any miracles. The attendance alone is probably going to be horrendous. None of the good math teachers wants the class. And we're only setting it up to keep a few of them in school a little longer to cut back on our dropout rate."

"There's more at stake here than the numbers that make us look bad because our kids quit school. We've got to make the course interesting enough for them to want to take it. And we should get the teacher who has the best, most positive attitude possible so we don't add to the problem we are trying to solve."

"Well, we're miles apart on this. I'm filling the roster with kids who are deficient in skills, frequently absent and not likely to graduate. If they make it . . . great. If not, at least we tried to make it easy enough for them to pass."

Schools shouldn't rationalize in that way and take the easy way out by diminishing standards in the hope that students will remain in school. The school's job is to make the school safe and to maintain standards of discipline and academic integrity. Students must master the three R's and much more. This is not an either/or situation. Districts must get serious about expectations and translate these expectations into standards in all schools. Citizens have a right to expect their institutions of learning to keep students in school and at the same time raise the academic bars of excellence. It will mean hard work and a constant focus on academic and behavioral discipline.

However, if schools choose the easy path of lowered standards because of a false approach to 'meeting the needs' or the fear of dropouts increasing, they will hurt the students they profess to serve.

Schools cannot control the environment outside their walls or in the home. Experienced educators realize that we live in an imperfect world and things are not as we wish them to be. Schools do face the fact that they are not going to get support from many homes and the neighborhoods are cruel and the values and attitudes of the street will work against the attitudes and values schools want to cultivate. Therefore the road to climb will be difficult. Yet better schools do the job of educating and do not make excuses for lack of performance.

If that doesn't happen, then students graduate with some momentary feeling of accomplishment, but feel a cruel sting of disappointment when they present themselves for employment and know that they haven't learned very much at all.

Chief executive officers of corporations, military leaders, and college presidents have said over and over again that students coming from many of our schools, especially in urban areas, do not have fundamental basic skills. One general told me: "We must give students oral instructions because we can't trust the kids to read a manual written at a ninth-grade level. They will mess up our expensive machinery." Industrial leaders say the same thing. New employees must be put in corporate classrooms to re-learn what they haven't mastered in the public schools. Corporate leaders tell me attitudes toward work, punctuality, and persistence are often poor.

That our system has failed so many students over the past two decades can also be seen in many of our colleges where students are accepted who haven't learned much from kindergarten through twelfth grade. The colleges, instead of excluding these students or accepting them on a trial basis for a year, fall into the same trap as the public schools. They accept remedial students, lower the standards, diminish the curriculum, inflate the grades, and pass students on.

In New Jersey, a move for accountability to determine whether college sophomores could pass a basic skills test was unanimously rejected by the college community. The argument was made that assessment was more than basic skills. Of course, assessment is more than basic skills, but that is no reason to avoid the issue of essential learning. In reality, *the fear of the colleges was that many students who gained entry under an 'open admissions' policy simply couldn't pass a basic skills test and the colleges might have had to come face to face with the issue of diminished standards.*

Former Governor Thomas Kean of New Jersey stated forcefully where he stood on the issue of standards and assessment. When he was the Governor, he said, "Some people have asked me to delay the new more academically rigorous high school graduation standards. They say that our children can't make it, that many children cannot learn to read and write and do arithmetic. Nonsense! I know our children have the ability to learn. The question is: do our schools have the capacity to teach?"

Governor Kean was right on target. Standards are necessary, but standards without the leadership to enable students to reach objectives renders raising the bar meaningless. The schools' attitude must be: "You can do it, and we will help you achieve."

In his book *Necessary Lessons: Decline and Renewal in American Schools,* Gilbert T. Sewell says: "Strong leadership is absolutely necessary for our schools to be effective."[4] He adds: "In good schools, the principals and department heads act as fierce guardians of instructional quality by standing for high academic outcomes. These administrators are willing to be unpopular, if necessary, in the cause of responsible schooling. They tend not to be permissive, informal in their staff relationships or overly interested in public relations."

Joseph Adelson, in an insightful *Commentary* magazine article,[5] quoted Herbert Walberg saying, "Given the will power, we have the ability to increase student learning." Adelson was very much interested in Walberg's use of the term WILLPOWER, a word we don't often see in print. He felt it was important because the people who run the schools, the board of education, administrators, and teachers must understand that willpower, purpose, and commitment are really required of them. In another essay for *Commentary,* Adelson used stinging words to press his point: "This country deserves far better public schools," he wrote, "but will get them only if we can find a way to cope with the intellectual inertia of our educational leadership."[6]

In all enterprises, leadership is a critical variable. If the people who have assumed leadership positions merely 'run the organization,' have low expectation, and little vision, commitment, or sense of purpose, then the schools will be poorly served. There is much that can and must be done to make schools better. We know a lot about what makes schools effective. Since we have this knowledge, there is no reason why schools should not focus on these characteristics of effectiveness.

- **Does the school or district focus more on the societal problems than on clear plans for educational improvement?**
- **Is the school's conversation about 'victims' and 'meeting individual needs' a cover-up for its shoddy planning and performance?**
- **Are rationalizations given for lowered behavioral and academic rigor?**
- **If the words of the school leadership support high standards, does the reality of planning, programs, and results meet the rhetoric?**

# 2
# How to Tell Good Teachers from Bad

**H**ere's the chance you've always wanted! Pretend for a moment that you can turn the tables and fill out a report card evaluating a teacher that your son or daughter had in class recently. The usual grades of A through F could be used for categories like:

Availability: _____
Involvement: _____
Concern and sensitivity: _____
Speed of homework and test correction: _____
Standards and expectations: _____
Directness in following curriculum: _____
Response to student feedback: _____
Organization and record keeping: _____

These are some of the issues that will be dealt with in this chapter. But before we delve into our consideration of faculty members, there's a special need here for an additional word of caution.

No parent in any country under any circumstances is ever completely indifferent to the personalities of the teachers entrusted with the care of their children. We don't have to look far for the historical reasons for such concern. In earlier years, when Latin was used to explain certain matters, a teacher was expected to act *in loco parentis*: 'in place of the parent.' Subsequently, moms and dads paid closer attention to individual teachers than to almost any other dimension of a young child's education.

Parents themselves recall their prolonged experiences with teachers in their own upbringings. Even those far removed from the realms of boards of education, superintendents, and school supervisors, have high or low estimations of faculty members. Those feelings sometimes say more about a parent's regard for their own scholastic backgrounds than about the staffs that educate their youngsters.

Therefore, because of tensions sometimes created in the parent-child-teacher relationship, it is extremely important in this chapter to deal frankly with many topics. Involvement, expectations, grades, staff development, and student feedback are all pivotal ingredients in understanding how teachers perform. Because they are on the firing line every day and most directly influence the attitudes of a child toward education itself, it is fair to say that teachers are in the single most important position within the realm of education. Let's now look at how to deal fairly with those who have what has been called "one of the most complicated jobs in the world."

## Teachers' Expectations

In almost every effective school, teachers who set and communicate high expectations to all their students obtain greater academic performance than teachers who set low expectations. The message of high expectation is, 'you can do it and I will help.' We may call it the Pygmalion effect or a self-fulfilling prophecy, but the idea of teachers really believing that students can and will learn has a most positive effect. Conversely, when teachers communicate to students that they cannot learn, this has an obvious—and negative—effect.

A friend of mine from Massachusetts told me how discouraged he had been by one of his high school teachers years earlier during his adolescence.

"In those days, Saul," he said, "many of the young Irish kids hanging out in the towns of Massachusetts could usually look forward to lives spent as city workers. Our fathers were right off the boats from places like Donegal or Dublin. They got jobs as cops, firemen, and bus drivers during the depression days and they were damned glad to have work at all."

"But they made you go to school," I interjected.

"Sure they sent us to schools, both Catholic and public. But not all the teachers had high hopes for us. When they deal with poor or immigrant children, lots of teachers figure it's an accomplishment just to take the edge off the accents kids use when speaking. Teaching such pupils to write well in a language their parents haven't mastered is doubly hard. So a lot of our teachers would just give up on us."

I thought briefly about what he said. Keep in mind here that I was hearing this from a man for whom I had great respect while we sat at a national conference where he was invited to address 49 other state commissioners of education. Clearly, I thought, the teachers of someone who would go on to enjoy the success and prestige of this individual would have detected his potential in adolescence. Surely anyone entrusted with encouraging the young would have tried to promote a pupil as motivated and as savvy as he must have been.

"These teachers weren't half bad," he continued. "Some just had little or no interest in picturing us as any more successful than our parents. And since most of our folks were bogged down without much education or visions of a better future, our scripts weren't going to call for many lead roles either. By the time I got to my senior year, my academic record was reasonably good but I was not directed towards anything other than work as a public employee or blue-collar laborer.

"One teacher told me to forget it when I asked about going on to college. She said I'd be smarter to make what money there was right away in a job I could find to help out with my family. And if I got really lucky, I could land a spot with the cops or post office or in the fire department. She said that that was what a student with my background should do."

The twinkle in my friend's eyes then turned from mild amusement to hurt. I could sense how much this insult had stung him as a boy whose visions included more than walking a beat. His pride informed him well and he knew, as I do, that it's fine to be a police officer or fire fighter. But it is also wrong for educators to tell young people what they ought to be and fail to challenge boys and girls in underprivileged families. Without condemning his school, he continued the account of his approach to manhood.

'I didn't give up on myself, mind you. But the Navy seemed a good choice to me then. I signed up, shipped out, and got along much better with superior officers than I had with so many of the faculty back in my home town."

My own experiences as commanding officer of the Navy Reserve Training center in Philadelphia made me think I knew exactly how he felt. I met dozens of recruits like him and tried my best to encourage them to use their new skills well. And many of them, having received from the Navy the recognition that they had missed previously, succeeded.

"So with the Navy's help I went on to continue my education and later became a teacher. My new self-confidence and sense of direction moved me then into administration. The success I enjoyed there prompted the Massachusetts State Board of Education to appoint me Commissioner in 1982. It was a job I relished because it gave me a chance to learn and grow and lead in a way that I wouldn't have if I settled for the life that someone else envisioned for me in my youth."

As I sat enraptured while listening to this story of his ups and downs, I thought of others whose ethnicity presented what foreigners perceive as obstacles to the American success story. All too often gifted children who are Latino, black, or Asian seem disadvantaged as they start the long climb up the academic ladder toward futures that their own parents may not have been able to contemplate in various professions. But however poor our national record on this issue may sometimes seem to outsiders, the truth remains that no other country on earth channels the downtrodden to the top as frequently or quickly as America. I've never met an educator who couldn't tell at least one story of a former student or friend who'd put incredible distances between the members of a single generation and their grandparents. So often does this occur, in fact, that teachers should be extremely wary of discouraging any child for fear of having someday to eat their words and apologize for not knowing better or to acknowledge and support their students' aspirations.

An African-American friend of mine dropped out of his high school because teachers told him that "kids like you should forget about academic achievement." Because of his determination, he ultimately got his diploma, graduated from college and now is an executive in a major New Jersey corporation.

On the other hand I know countless people who have told me that "if it weren't for a teacher, counselor, or coach, I never would have made it. They believed in me when I didn't believe in myself."

Expectations of adults have a powerful affect on the young. Good schools are nurturing institutions where the adults sincerely believe that their attitude, enthusiasms, caring, and expectations will have much to do with their students' success.

> • **What expectations do your teachers have for their students? How do they communicate these expectations to students?**

## Courses of Study

The course of study (fourth grade science, sixth grade math, Spanish I, Algebra II . . . ) should list the *objectives* to be taught, the *standards* of acceptable student learning, and the method of *assessing* learning. It should be very specific and easy to read. It should not contain the various ways a teacher might choose to teach. Those decisions are the individual teachers' to make. Courses of study, if written correctly, should not exceed 10 pages.

*Parents can determine if their schools are really serious about academic excellence by examining the courses of study,* which can be one of the most powerful tools for your child's learning. Unfortunately, that is seldom the case. In many school districts, a course of study is written by a single teacher, or two or three teachers as a 'summer project.' These courses of study often have no consistency, subject to subject or grade level to grade level. They reflect the ideas and biases of the teacher or teachers who wrote them. Frequently they are 30, 50, or 80 pages and at their worst, do nothing more than paraphrase the contents, sample test questions, and resources listed in the textbook. They are something to have on hand to show a visiting committee or a parent. "Yes, we do have a course of study and yes, they are revised every five years." In reality, the very vehicle (course of study) which should determine what is to be taught, is routinely ignored by most teachers in most schools!

How can this happen? Quite easily. Many schools boards and administrators treat the courses of study with benign neglect. What should be a critical aspect of your child's schooling is often treated in a cavalier manner. Written as something to 'get done,' the course of study gives parents the perception of a blueprint for children's instruction when, in reality, none exists.

This may sound like an academic freedom issue—'You mean a teacher can't teach what he/she feels is best'—but this is so only on a superficial level. Clear and uniform ends can plainly spell out what will be taught. Clear objectives, specific standards, and concluding assessment procedures are written into a good course of study. If this were not so, then a third-grade teacher who did not like to teach science would teach little science. Another third-grade teacher may not emphasize social studies, but will spend considerable time on science. When students of these teachers get to the fourth grade, one does not know much science and the other not much social studies. The fourth-grade teacher, if she is capable in science and social studies, may say, "You must have had Mr. Smith because he doesn't like to teach much about social studies," or, "You probably had Miss Brown because she doesn't like to do the work having to do with electricity, weather, and metamorphosis."

Some agreement on what objectives are to be reached and what the standards are will let us determine acceptable learning for the students. Finally, schools need to state how student learning will be assessed, so that everyone will know whether pupils have reached the standards in relation to the objectives.

Many parents have complained that by the time their child reached the eighth or ninth grade, they had been taught certain concepts three or four times. This is usually the result of poor planning and co-ordination within schools, not careful reinforcement of critical concepts.

Education is not a random affair. Teachers have the absolute right, but also the obligation, to work with their administration in order to establish the objectives for every course and subject. For example, schools must state the objectives of the second-grade science program, the third-grade science program, and the fourth-grade science program. Administrators can then show the standards which will demonstrate whether the students have met the objective. Assessments will determine whether these standards have been reached. The public will then see measurable ways of knowing that the intended content is actually learned. Let's give teachers the authority *and* hold them responsible. That's what professionalism is about.

How can we do that? Really quite simply. Assume a kindergarten through sixth-grade school; the teachers in grades K through 6 will work in teams with a consultant and/or subject matter expert to determine the specific objectives of the science, social studies, math, and reading programs. The resultant courses of study should be clear and direct. They should state the objectives, standards, and method of assessment which will determine what the students learned.

Since most assessment is done through testing, these formal grade level and subject matter tests are then constructed by the teachers and given at least twice during the school year. Accurate records will show which questions were answered correctly and which were not. Such information will help teachers understand which concepts were well-taught and which were not. Students and parents will receive specific information on how well students have learned with respect to what is most important for them to learn.

When the district-wide tests are given in third-grade math or fourth-grade science, these results inform the board of education and the public. Are the children learning? Where are the problems? What improvements are needed? If the primary purpose of school is the academic development of the children, then there is nothing more important than the question, "Are the children learning what they are supposed to learn?"

This same approach holds true for all subjects whether in the middle school, the junior high, or the high school. The teachers who instruct in United States History I, Algebra II, or Biology need to convey in a clear and unambiguous manner the objectives, standards, and the assessment for their specific subject. The subject matter expert—the science department chairperson, social studies department chairperson, or the university expert may also help the classroom teachers write the courses of study.

**There is no reason why courses of study cannot be distributed to parents at the beginning of every school year.** Why shouldn't the school say to a parent, "This is what we teach, these are our objectives, these are the standards, and this how we will assess." Schools should say to parents: "Here is your road map. Here is your guide to what is going on. We want to share this with you so you will know, in *understandable terms*, exactly what we are going to do this year in this subject to help your child."

Since the parents and teachers will have the same course of study, any conferences between parents and teachers will start off at a more professional level because everyone will know what is being required. The same holds true in elementary school or high school. If a student is studying Algebra II, Biology, U.S. History I, or Sociology, there is no reason why the course of study shouldn't be sent home at the beginning of the school year so that the parents know what to expect.

Teachers emphasize different topics in their classes. Some cover more of the textbook while others teach in-depth with supplementary materials. While, on one hand, we can respect the teachers' decision-making and flexibility within the classroom, their discretion ideally exists only within the context of the course or subject objectives. Only when these are clear can parents have reasonable assurance that each teacher is following a clear road map (course of study) for their son's or daughter's experience during that particular year.

When this occurs, not only is teaching more focused and co-ordinated grade-to-grade, but testing gives the public school board, parents, administration, and teachers a clear picture of what is learned. Test questions written by the faculty and targeted to the objectives and standards will answer the question, 'Are the children learning?'

Why isn't this done? Because it is easier to let everyone do what they desire than to buckle down and get fundamental academic issues straight. What I am saying to do is not difficult to achieve—good schools are doing it. The tragedy is that something so easy to achieve is not being done in many of our schools. This works to the detriment of children.

- **What do the courses of study look like in your schools? Are they specific with respect to objectives, standards, and assessment? When were they last modified? Who modified them? Do they serve as the basis for classroom instruction? How do you know?**
- **Are the results of grade level exams (third grade science) and the subject matter tests (Algebra II) made public?**

# Grading

Courses of study that act as a constant guide to teachers help them with their weekly and daily planning ('lesson plans'). Courses of study also enable teachers to ensure that their quizzes and exams are more consistent with respect to objectives. But no matter how well the course objectives, standards, and assessment measures are laid out, inconsistencies in the grading structure of individual teachers remain.

The problems are obvious, but most school districts do little about them. Miss Jones gives Robert an A in third-grade math. He moves into fourth grade and Miss Smith gives him a C in math. Miss Smith says that Miss Jones is an "easy market" and doesn't push the children particularly hard, while she is more rigorous and gives tougher tests.

The parents are confused. Is their son a good math student or a bad math student? Is the C in one class worth as much or more than the A in the other class?

One teacher may grade on a curve (10 percent A, 20 percent B, 40 percent C, 20 percent D, 10 percent F) and even if the students haven't learned too much, a certain percentage will get A's. Another teacher may grade on the percentage right and wrong and nobody will get an A, even though the test was more rigorous and many students knew more than the students who got an A under the 'curve' grading method.

A school's grading policy should be clear to everyone. That policy may set certain boundaries such as 'homework will count for 10 percent of the final grade and exams and quizzes will count for at least 60 percent. Grading of all exams and quizzes will be on a standard curve or percentage basis. Each teacher at the beginning of the school year will state their grading approach within these limits'). This tells everyone—the student, the parents, and the community—that grading is carefully thought through and a consistent position is taken that applies to everyone.

This brings me to the level of classroom testing. Whatever the grading system, Mr. Johnson or Ms. Greene will give tests to students periodically to see whether they have learned the material. Parents and citizens should determine if the administration is very careful with respect to teachers' 'reviewing' before the test.

There is certainly nothing wrong with the teacher touching on the most important points which he thinks students ought to know for a major test. However, there is plenty wrong with a teacher saying, 'This is what I am going to ask you on the test tomorrow, so you should study it tonight' or, 'Better know about X, Y, and Z. I'll ask it on the test.' Of course, the students do exactly what is required. They force-feed themselves the information the night before and forget it just as quickly after the test. The student learns very quickly to memorize only what the teacher reviews the day before the test. This approach makes a mockery out of what students should do—master the essential facts, understand concepts and ideas, infer, deduce, and have their minds stretched by a good teacher. A teacher should say to the student: 'If you have learned well, you can apply what you learned to the questions on this test.'

All too frequently some teachers rely exclusively on short-answer tests, ones that use true-or-false, fill-in-the-blank, and matching questions. Often these are given because they are easy to correct and grade. Yet they lead students toward a mind-set of a specific correct answer and the student thinks: "What is the teacher going to ask on this particular test? Does this look like a fill-in-the-blank or potential true/false question?" In situations such as these, the student is not really assimilating the knowledge and understanding that was taught, but trying to play the game of cat and mouse with the teacher.

*Make certain that teachers give essay questions on all measures of assessment.* This type of test takes longer to grade, but is so important to the students' best interests. **Students can and should write with comfort as early as the first grade.** The world is not true or false questions, multiple choice, or matching columns. Students need to put facts together, to deduce from facts, to argue various viewpoints, and to predict outcomes. So parents must ask: "Are essay questions required as a form of assessment? How many essay questions are given on a particular test? What percentage of tests given are essay questions?"

*When tests are given, are they returned promptly?* Too often, a test is given one week and not returned until two or three weeks later. This does both teacher and student a disservice. Students do not find out immediately what they have mastered and what they have not. It is not helpful for students to have a test returned and analyzed if they are now two weeks into new material. The only importance of the test in this situation is to see what grade was obtained.

If the test is returned immediately, the student finds out what he doesn't know and has a chance to learn the material before moving on. The teachers, if they correct the paper immediately, know what the students learned and what the students did not learn. If several students have failed to demonstrate understanding of a critical concept, this indicates to the teacher that some re-teaching in particular areas is needed before moving ahead.

- **Is there a policy on grading? Is it consistently applied?**
- **Are teachers' tests corrected and returned promptly?**
- **Are essay questions always given?**

# Organization and Effectiveness

Good teachers are organized. They set clear goals for students and make certain that students understand the goals. Students are aware when their teacher is presenting each day's lesson in a very carefully planned way. These assignments are not haphazard and thrown together at the last minute. The students know when they are going into the class of an effective teacher because there is evidence of preparation every single day. In turn, students expect more of themselves.

An organized teacher never forgets what the assignment was or what homework is expected. The teacher is well aware of where the class ended its work yesterday and picks up that thread quickly. The class starts on time and the students are immediately involved in the lesson. Students are given clear and concise explanations of sequences and the illustrations that the teacher uses are the result of careful thought and planning—no flying by the seat of the pants! The examples, the illustrations, the use of the overhead projector, or the slides used are carefully organized to fit into the teacher's presentation.

A good teacher does not show a film that has little to do with the lesson. The weak teacher does, and is always looking for ways to let the kids and himself 'have a break.' The students understand this all too well.

The prepared and effective teacher asks frequent questions to see if students understand their work, and does not plunge on until it is clear that the students understand. It does no good to give a scholarly lecture for forty minutes only to learn during the last five minutes of the period that the students have understood nothing. The organized and effective teacher actively engages all of the students and does not make the mistake of calling upon the same upraised hands time after time. Calling on the same individuals may give the teacher the impression that everyone understands what is taught when that is not the case. Good teachers ask difficult questions, not always simple recall questions. Facts are important but facts are most valuable when they enable students to support concepts, build arguments, and evaluate the assertions of others.

Most of the facts that one learns, whether in Biology or History, are forgotten within a short period of time. If anyone wants to prove this in a school setting, all they need do is give seniors the final exam in the Biology course they took as sophomores. If those exams were based on fact and recall knowledge, you would find the majority of students failing the tests. Organized and effective teachers use fact as a starting point, not as an ending point. They ask students, 'Why do you think that? Can you see the situation from the other side? What do you think will happen next?'

In the Introduction I mentioned an experience I had teaching about the Panama Canal. Later that first year of teaching I had a similar experience in an economics class. I had dutifully 'taught' the facts of the Sherman Act, the Clayton Act, and other legislation that dealt with monopolies, competition, and restraint of trade. The students read the information in the text and I asked true/false, fill-in-the-blank, and matching type of recall questions. The students obediently regurgitated back to me what I asked. Yet the shock occurred again: three months later, no one knew the Sherman from the Clayton Act.

I changed things radically the following year. Students still had to know the facts but instead of dwelling on them in detail, I had the students learn the essence of the major legislation rather quickly. I was surprised at how quickly they learned, by my force-feeding them and promising them an exciting activity.

With some Cecil B. DeMille hoopla, I gave students a case study. I had carefully arranged a situation where a major American manufacturer wanted to take over a coffee company of medium size. I composed background information on the major company and the coffee company and presented facts that were important and facts that were of no importance to the issues of competition and restraint of trade. I brought in actual issues and court decisions that applied to the specific case study and some which had very little application.

I asked the class to read the background material during one evening and the class discussed it during the next class period. Then, the next night, I asked the students to read the case itself, and to come prepared to discuss whether the major company could legally take over the coffee company.

The class was divided into five groups of approximately five students apiece. They had two class periods to make a decision with respect to whether the one company could or could not take over the other. Each group had to support their decision according to the law and prior decisions. It was interesting to note that midway through the first day three of the independent groups asked me if I would be available after school because they wanted to work on the case. (This had never happened before!)

Suffice to say, I was amazed when each group did an outstanding job. Almost everyone in class thought hard about the situation. They argued about what was relevant fact and what was not, why something was important or why it was irrelevant. How did the Sherman Act, the Clayton Act, and the other acts apply to this particular case?

After two days of work, the students made outstanding presentations. Since each group was involved in the process, they chuckled at the other groups' 'ineptness,' or what they thought were errors in reasoning. At times, they had to admit that the other groups had spotted things which they had missed.

This type of activity involved *every* student. They had to know facts, understand the law, examine prior cases, argue, and finally come to a conclusion. Then, they had to listen to others who may have come to conclusions with logic that was equal to or exceeded theirs.

How different from the often-used 'book report' activity! In that approach, day after day, students report on the book they have read. Other students are lulled into sleep because they have not read that particular book—they have only read their book. The teacher justifies this terrible approach because each student has to 'organize and present.' And everyone else sits bored as can be. This is 'teaching' at its worst. There is almost no exchange between the teacher and student and little, if any, between students. Yet, some teachers persist in this 'activity' at the rate of 4/5 students each day, wasting at least a week of each child's potential learning time.

It should be clear that activities involving the total class are preferable to those with little involvement. Yet, teachers often persist in the book report activity, at the expense of more fruitful activities such as the case study.

It is very hard for a parent or citizen to know what is happening in the classroom. Parents get their information secondhand, often in bits and pieces, from students, administrators, or the teachers themselves.

***You can ask your principal or teacher to see teachers' lesson plans for the past month.*** These plans detail the daily objectives, the process to reach the objectives, homework, and assessment. Although 'required' of each teacher, they are seldom, if ever, reviewed by the principals. By your asking to see the lesson plans, you exert subtle pressure on principals and teachers.

***If these daily plans are carefully constructed and are consistent with the course of study, then the teacher is a real professional who has prepared for the job in a thorough manner. However, if plans are not in existence or are presented as hastily written notes, the teacher has done little preparation.***

The assessment, most often the tests, will give another clue to the teacher's thoroughness. ***Well-thought-out questions that go beyond recall will let you know if the test is a carefully-constructed academic exercise or a few recall questions from the questions at the end of the chapter in the textbook.***

- **Are your school's teachers organized for each day's lessons? Are the lessons carefully planned or written hurriedly minutes before the class begins?**
- **Are the teaching aids (slides, illustrations from magazines, reproduced quotes from novels, and so forth) carefully integrated into lessons?**
- **Is the entire class involved in the daily lesson or are lectures, book reports, and responding to a few extended hands the norm?**
- **Does the teacher use facts as a means to an end and not always an end in itself? Are the tests and quizzes short answer recall or exercises that make students organize and present knowledge in a coherent fashion?**

# Writing

Writing is critical, whether given as an assignment or in the testing situation. Good writing assignments are an extension of class reading and discussion, not isolated exercises. ***Students should begin their writing in the first grade and writing should be part of the daily work of the teacher and student. There should be major checkpoints in each of the grades where students are stretched to write more and to write better.*** The library must be used, not visited, in students' writing experiences. Essay questions are needed to test student understanding. Whether it is an assignment or an essay question on a test, this is the difference between a student knowing facts and the ability to *use* facts in a coherent way.

I mentioned that students can begin writing in Grade l. If we, as adults, have a strong will to teach children to write, they will write. If we have the will to see that students think, and not just memorize and regurgitate, they will think. Three-, four-, and five-year-olds repeatedly ask 'why' questions, and eagerly respond to questioning when adults read to them. When 'why' questions follow 'what' questions the young children are eager to offer their thoughts. As adults, we must free their natural curiosity by encouraging inquisitiveness and not squashing it beneath the tyranny of true and false queries or fill-in-the-blank questions.

Teachers in the elementary schools need to use writing assignments in science and social studies as well as language arts. This approach of writing across the disciplines flourishes if continued in the upper grades. Everyone becomes a teacher of grammar and composition, not only the teacher of English.

There should be evidence of whether this is happening in the writing assignments that are given each year to students. Essay questions in all disciplines allow writing instruction to become a team effort.

Educators are now weighing the long term advantages of keeping portfolios for each child. The idea is still too new for its full potential to be appreciated or evaluated critically. Proponents are suggesting that schools re-orient their procedures to make sure that portfolios contain important and significant examples of students' written work. They believe that portfolios and exhibits of students' work should replace dependence on tests, which they consider to be less indicative of the students' accomplishments.

Can professionals decide on the standards to be achieved in each grade and discipline? What constitutes satisfactory work, outstanding work? How will consistency and objectivity be established? Will portfolios and exhibitions result in students being able to write better?

- **Does your school have a specific approach to writing? What assignments are required at each grade level? How many assignments are given? What is the quality of the students' work?**
- **How important is the library with respect to students obtaining information?**
- **Are essay questions given on teacher tests? How often? Are they promptly returned? Do all high school teachers aid the instruction of writing?**
- **If your school is moving in the direction of portfolios and exhibitions as a method of assessment, how are standards determined? How is consistency determined within a grade and between grades? Do children write more? Write better?**

# Homework

The ambitious teacher gives thoughtful homework assignments. These reinforce what is going on in the classroom by extending and challenging the student to use what is learned in different ways, to see the assignment in a different light. For example, if the discussion in English deals with a certain aspect of Jim's character in the book, *Lord Jim*, perhaps the homework assignment could come at the reading selection from a difference angle. The author may be stressing the weakness of Lord Jim. Perhaps the teacher could ask, 'Do you see any strength in Jim's character to this point?' (The teacher might limit the homework assignment to 200 words in order to facilitate correction.)

Most junior high school and high school math teachers give dull homework assignments. 'Do problems 2, 4, 6, 8, and 10 at the end of this chapter,' says the teacher. Sound familiar? Less familiar is the imaginative and rigorous assignment of 'Mr. Mitchell's Problem of the day' that I mentioned in chapter 1. Mr. Mitchell gave one tough problem each day, reviewed it in class and corrected it that very evening.

If homework isn't corrected quickly, it is of limited value. Most 'workers' at any age want to know that their 'boss' is observant with respect to their work. When someone says 'good job,' they want to know that the boss has looked closely at their work and it merits praise. *If teachers do not correct homework promptly, its value is greatly diminished.*

Principals and teachers at one school I know of showed that they meant what they said they meant about homework. They enforced the policy by monitoring the doors at dismissal and sending empty-handed students back to their rooms to get their homework. Parents were informed if students were not completing their homework assignments, and those students were retained after lunch, during recess, or after school in the homework center to complete the missing assignments.

At times schools will buy 'learning materials' that are forever 'stored' in closets and drawers, and spend money on 'credits' accumulated by staff that have little relevance to student learning. Yet, imaginatively assigned homework, which is corrected promptly, has great academic value to students. According to the eminent scholar Herbert Walberg, homework is a strong predictor of student learning. Homework has a high payoff to students and the increased costs are zero.

Isn't it interesting that boards, administrators, and teachers often focus on that which has high costs to the taxpayer and little value to students rather than the reverse?

- **What is your school's policy vis-à-vis homework? Is the policy followed at the classroom level? What is the quality of the homework? Is it corrected and returned to the student promptly? How do you know?**

# After School

Part of a teacher's job is to help the students, and that means to give assistance beyond the classroom. Teachers will many times ask students to give extra effort. Look in your schools to see if teachers are also doing this. ***How many teachers and students stay after school each day?***

Almost fifty percent of our students now in school will spend some part of their school years with one parent only. Students often need their mother or father to talk with, and in many situations that parent is not there. Even if a junior high school or high school has excellent guidance counselors, this does not serve the purpose of having someone available when a student needs them.

Guidance counselors have multiple responsibilities and are not always available to a student when that student needs help. Also, a student is much more likely to turn to a teacher they respect than to a guidance counselor they have seen once or twice. Counselors are often warm and caring persons, but they rarely have daily contact with students prior to crises.

If a teacher exudes warmth and lets the students know that she really cares about them as individuals, then students may wish to stay after school to talk. The conversation will go far beyond the algebraic equation which they didn't understand, and perhaps center on problems that they are having at home, with a friend, or possibly with drugs.

As a teacher grades students, students 'grade' teachers. Students know if a teacher is warm, accessible, enthusiastic, and caring. If the teacher exhibits these types of human traits, students will seek the teacher's counseling and advice. Many teachers are fond of saying: 'I teach students. Then, I teach students biology.' When this really occurs the students know the teachers care about them personally and they turn naturally to these teachers as role models.

Frequently it is the teacher who will say to the student, 'Mary, you look a little down today,' or 'Mary, your work seems to be slipping a little bit. Come in after school and let's talk about it.' Another teacher knows a student's mother and father have recently separated. He says: 'Pete, I know that you hurt your foot and won't be able to play basketball for the team next week; why don't you stop in after school since you can't practice and let's talk.' If the rapport between student and teacher is positive and the student grapevine says that the teacher is a 'good guy,' Mary and Pete will respond.

How many teachers stay after school in your school building? Many times teachers will say, 'I am available if the student asks.' But that is a dodge. No one is going to ask to see a teacher after school if they know that all of the 'vibrations' given off by the teacher are saying, 'I've got more important things to do after school then to stay and be accessible to you.' If everything in the teacher's interaction with the student is saying, 'Don't ask me to stay after school,' than words which say, 'I'm available' mean next to nothing.

I know of school districts where teachers have negotiated with the school board to stay after school one day each week for thirty minutes! The students get the message. If the teachers negotiated to stay after 'school only one day a week for thirty minutes, then it's clear to them that the teachers really don't care. In one school district the teachers post 'their days' to stay after school. The ridiculousness of this approach is readily apparent. If a student does not understand his assignment on Tuesday, but the teacher only stays after school on Monday, the student must wait six days until he or she can get help. The assistance is needed immediately, not five or six days later. It's no wonder that private tutors are doing a great business in this district.

Students seldom volunteer to stay after school for academic help. When teachers post one day a week that they are available, it is no surprise when nobody comes. The atmosphere in the school must say, 'We are learners here. If you aren't doing well, please ask to stay. We want you to ask and we want to help you. We'll see that after school we give the help to improve your grades.'

Most suburban schools have a bus available for athletes two hours after school ends. They should budget for a similar bus for the students who have academic problems or other personal needs.

Some teachers will say that what I have written to this point is not balanced. They will say, 'I don't make enough money and I must leave after school to take my second job.' I would like to see higher teacher salaries and all excellent teachers well paid. Having said this, I know some people will need or want extra dollars and wish to hold a second job. That is their right and no one can tell them what to do. As long as their performance in the classroom is satisfactory or better, the school district has no right to tell anyone what they can do with their extra time. However, the school district has every right to tell teachers that they may not leave school until 30 or 45 minutes after the last class. The second job cannot become a priority. The students' learning and personal needs are the priority.

- **How many of your students stay after school for extra academic help? How many of your teachers are in their classrooms for at least a half an hour every day after school?**
- **How many of your schools have a late bus one hour after school for students who need extra academic help?**

# Communication with Parents

Parents want to know how their children are doing in school and it is the responsibility of the schools to keep parents informed. Frequently, this communication centers around report cards, conferences, and back-to-school nights.

The primary vehicle for communication is often the impersonal report card. I have already commented on grading and courses of study, so that parents have a better idea of how to understand grades and what it means with respects to the subject content.

In many elementary schools, conferences between parents and teachers are held in addition to, or in place of, report cards. These conferences are from twenty to thirty minutes in length with parents tightly scheduled one after the other. Like a physician 'examining' the entire soccer team in one hour, the teacher moves quickly from one parent to the other.

These conferences are frequently of little value. The teacher will try to keep tight control of the conference and touch only on those items which the principal or union regard as safe. Parents will struggle to expand the 'agenda' to topics they wish to pursue.

Conferences are scheduled at specific times during the year. This is often counter to the students' interest, because a conference is necessary when the student is having a problem, not two months later, when a twenty-minute conference is scheduled. Yet principals and teachers will often discourage parents who ask for a conference because they are concerned with their child's learning. 'The fall conference is scheduled for a few weeks—why don't you bring it up then?' is often a principal's or teacher's comment to parents.

If conferences are held at fixed times, not when parents see the need, or if they are scheduled for twenty-minute 'blocks' one after the other, then why do parents attend conferences in such numbers? The answer lies at the heart of the problem; since there is often little meaningful communication, parents will take what they can get.

It's the same reason that many attend back-to-school nights. They want that thirty minutes with the elementary school teacher or ten minutes with each high school teacher. Maybe they can ask a question or two on the way in or out of the classroom about *their* child's needs. Perhaps they can ask one question about content, writing, grading, or special projects after the teachers have finished their presentations to the parents.

The system is often organized to discourage the very communications the bureaucracy says it wants to occur. Conferences that are fixed and predetermined give the illusion of open communication when, in reality, they discourage it. Packed sardine tight into twenty- to thirty-minute blocks, parents seldom have an opportunity for substantive two-way conversation. Back-to-school night is another illusion. Harmless in itself, it does nothing more than give a parent a few minutes to listen to what the teacher says about the academic offerings.

There is a simple way to improve all this. First, schedule conferences on a 'needs' basis. When parents or teachers feel there is something to discuss, they should meet. The conversation will be appropriate to the child when the particular problem or opportunity occurs. **When a parent calls, the school staff ought to respond quickly and well.** If Mrs. Jones wants to see Teacher Smith about Tommy's behavior or grades, the secretary should be able to schedule the conference at that time. (She knows that Teacher Smith will see parents on Tuesday morning from 7:30 to 8:00 A.M. or after school on Wednesday from 3:00 to 3:45 P.M. or 3:45 to 4:30 P.M.) Likewise, if a teacher wants to see a parent, Teacher Smith asks the secretary to 'schedule a conference with Mrs. Jones about Tommy's work during the time that I am available for conferences.'

If the school board and administration want their schools to be open to parents, these contacts will happen. Anyone can then check to see **how many parents call to see teachers and how many conferences are held.** Anyone can also check to see **how many teachers called parents and how many conferences are held.**

In high schools very few teacher conferences take place. Teachers frequently argue that a fourteen-to-eighteen-year-old has responsibilities to discuss issues with his parents. I agree, but this does not let the teacher off the hook with respect to contacting parents when necessary. However, this is seldom done. 'I have 125 students. Do you expect me to contact and conference with even half of my students?' teachers ask. Of course not: a good teacher has many responsibilities, as I have

mentioned in this chapter, but, only ten to twenty of the
have problems that necessitate a conference. A teac
100–125 students and it is not realistic to see every pareni.
not be used as an umbrella excuse for seeing none!

The same procedure I mentioned before can be used by a parent or
teacher to set up a conference through the school secretary. Because a
student is fifteen or sixteen doesn't mean he is an adult and totally
responsible for his actions. If teachers will regularly reach out to parents and parents know that teachers are responsive, students will
benefit.

Principals and superintendents tell me that many parents report that
after they had met with high school teachers and asked that they be
kept informed about their child, teachers did not keep their promises.
Because this complaint continues to be made to me by parents of high
school students, it prompts me to make note of it.

If parents see high school teachers and promises are made to keep
parents informed, those promises become part of a trust as well as a
public relations issue. Parents should tell the principal, superintendent,
and board if promises are not kept. And the principal, superintendent,
and board must deal firmly with the teachers involved. They must also
see to it that no retribution of any kind finds its way back to the student.
As always, the 'system' must serve the student and no one else.

On the positive side, but clearly an exception, one elementary
teacher I know sends notes home to parents every month. They are
informative and often praiseworthy. At times, they ask the parents'
help. It's true that this teacher has only twenty-five students, but the
same point can be made when the teacher has 50 or 125. Perhaps, only
twenty to thirty parents need notices each month. How much time does
it take to write twenty or thirty memos each month?

Another teacher I know calls the parents of each student twice each
year. She teaches one hundred students! If the student is doing well, the
parent will hear it from the teacher. If a youngster is having a small
problem, the teacher will mention it and say, 'I need your help. Could
you review his work for the next few weeks to ensure it is complete?'
This teacher tells me it takes her an average of three minutes per call.
Parents are so startled to hear from her that they usually say, 'Thank
you for taking the time to call—thank you for caring about my son.'
With her hundred students the total time expended is five hours twice
each year.

- **What do your schools or teachers do with respect to communication between teacher and parent? Are twenty-minute conferences the routine two or three times each year in your elementary schools?**
- **How many conferences are held when needed? Who initiated them—parent or teacher?**
- **Does your administration foster a solid, open approach or do the words and the deeds not match? Do teachers reach out to parents with notes and phone calls? Is the administration and teaching staff responsive to parents? How do you know?**

# Involvement

Teachers have great latitude in the day-to-day operation of their class-rooms. Yet this autonomy often results in isolation. In some schools, two teachers teaching the same subject or within the same department may seldom speak to each other about instructional issues and it is not uncommon for situations such as this to exist for years. Like neighbors with an invisible fence, two teachers may make small talk, but never sit down with each other to discuss issues of substance.

What are some of these issues? There is the necessity for specific objectives, standards, and assessment procedures in each subject area in the elementary schools and discrete subject areas in high schools (biology, chemistry). The teachers are the instructional experts and, therefore, must be involved in this regard. It is wrong to impose a final 'product' without the involvement and suggestions of the people responsible for its implementation.

I will discuss in the next chapter the critical responsibility of the principal to supervise teachers as they instruct children. Principals should supervise and evaluate teachers based upon criteria that reflect excellence in teaching. That leads to the question, 'just what is excellent teaching?'

The answer, fortunately, is reasonably clear and research findings will lead schools along similar paths of definition. But it is important that teachers are involved in this process of inquiry and definition. When they are, the results are more strongly supported and not just tolerated.

There are many curriculum issues that cross grade levels and schools. These 'linkage issues' are most important if the school organization is to function effectively. They influence teachers' lives so teachers should help resolve them. There should be an instructional council in the school district with its majority from the faculty ranks. The council's responsibility is to define instructional problems and resolve them.

Frequently, the administration or the board fears that this committee, which has district-wide responsibilities, will allow a teachers' union to pursue its agenda, to the detriment of students. I believe we should trust people's better motives and not fail to initiate because of things that could go wrong. If, after a district-wide curriculum committee is formed and it is apparent that the union is trying to cause mischief, then the administration can act. Many times they will find the union will act responsibly on instructional issues.

Why not bring teachers, administrators, and board members together? Conduct a climate inventory which measures everyone's opinions with respect to such areas as priorities, working conditions, communications, and teamwork. Where results show that there are significant problems, the board, administration, and teachers should try to agree on the issues that need their immediate attention as well as on a plan of action they will implement. By bringing the board, administrators, and teachers together in a professional way, the goal of truly effective schools becomes attainable. It is a lot better than having people work at cross purposes.

- **Are teachers involved in critical instructional issues? Are there interschool and district-wide curriculum committees? When major instructional problems face the district of school, are teachers part of the team searching for solutions?**
- **Who determines the criteria for evaluating teachers? Are teachers involved in this important area?**
- **Are courses of study revised by the best teachers, according to the guidelines mentioned earlier under 'Courses of Study'?**

## Staff Development

Educators are in the business of instruction and they understand how students learn. Yet, when it comes to the continued development of teachers, educators operate as if they do not know how learning takes place. The approach is at best haphazard, at worst nonexistent.

Teacher staff development falls primarily within three major categories—course credits at universities, conferences, and in-service days.

At best, graduate degrees wIthin a teacher's subject area may be of some use. I say 'may' because the advanced degree is often in such depth that its utility is far beyond that of an elementary or high school student.

More often, credits are accumulated for the singular purpose of a teacher reaching 30 or 45 credits beyond the bachelor's degree. When this occurs, the teacher gets more money on the salary scale, *yet there is no evidence that this approach yields any benefit to students.*

Even though credit accumulation is a costly practice with no student payoff, even worse are the one- and two-day 'seminars' that offer course credits. Usually affiliated with colleges that need extra revenues, these boiler operations have devised an interesting scheme. They offer a two-day seminar for 'two credits.' The college gets its 'cut' and the seminar organizer gets his. The teacher presents the credits as given by 'X' college. After attending a few of these seminars the teacher accumulates 30 additional credits and advances on the salary guide. A teacher with ten years' experience and a Bachelor's Degree makes $40,000. With the same years' experience, a Bachelor's Degree and 30 credits, he makes $45,000. And every subsequent year the teacher will make $5,000 a year additional because he 'gathered' 30 credits. Payoff to students: zero!

Conferences, at best, may help instruction. If carefully selected and matched to the needs of students, a conference will enable teachers to learn new techniques which might benefit students. At worst, conferences give teachers a break from the routine, and act as rewards dispensed in a now-it's-your-turn-to-go approach. With no attempt to define student needs and match the best teachers to the conference, the approach does not have student learning as its focus. There is no expectation that what was learned at a conference is intended for the classroom. The conference is seldom part of a comprehensive plan of a particular teacher development that will result in greater student learning. If you want to check this out, **ask the principal for a list of the conferences each teacher has attended for the past three years. Ask to see how this is part of a teacher's written comprehensive development plan and finally ask the principal if she has observed the teacher using the knowledge gained.**

The third approach is the so called 'in-service' days. In some districts these aren't even days, but a two-hour period for faculty to learn and thereby help students. In New Jersey and some other states if students attend school for four hours it is a 'legal day.' Since most states have a minimum number of days children must attend school (usually 180) a *full* day for teachers 'in-service' means that the day cannot count toward the 180 since the children weren't in school. However, if the children attend school from 8:00 A.M. to noon, it is a legal day! Then, after lunch, from approximately 1:00 P.M. to 3:00 P.M. teachers have 'in-service.' Tragically, the two-hour 'in-service day' is chosen over the full day because the two-hour approach allows the school to count the four-hour school day as a legal day.

This sleight of hand gives the appearance of real staff development when none exists. Such a pseudo approach to staff development is damaged even more when one knows what goes on in most 'in-service' days. At best, the 'in-service' approach is constructed with a clear objective based on student needs. The year's 'in-service' days (or hours) are connected so that what was accomplished in October is extended and reinforced in December and February. Unfortunately, that is seldom the way it works.

In many situations a problem or objective is stated and a dynamic speaker or panel addresses the issues. Teachers are interested and enthusiastic, but no follow-up or follow-through takes place. The faculty has had their consciousness raised, but that's it. What's in it for students? Very little. Even worse are 'in-service' days (hours) devoted to each school catching up on administrative chores, with very little pretense made of student problems, objectives, or the like.

If you want to see that what I have written is so, ***ask your school or school district to go back five years and to show you what transpired during the 'in-service' days.*** You will see, in the majority of situations, that there is no yearly plan, but absence of planning. There is little continuity year to year, but rather an approach that resembles a smorgasbord of unconnected offerings. There is no follow-through to ensure that what is learned is applied in the classroom.

I've sketched a dark picture and I've done so for two reasons. First, it's true. Second, good staff development is so important. All successful organizations invest in their people. The military trains all of the time and it is not unusual for people in industry to spend weeks each year learning and training. Many large corporations have their own 'universities.' and the learning is not haphazard or disparate. The corporation wants to ensure that what is taught meets a need of the organization and what is learned is soon applied.

Doctors, lawyers, accountants, electricians—all may leave the workplace to study. Whether it is in formal study, conferences or seminars, what is learned is soon applied. Only in the very business that knows how people learn do we do such a sloppy job planning our own growth!

Staff development is very important and we do it very poorly. But schools could improve quickly. To do so, they should list critical objectives which grow out of the problems schools have or the opportunities that are before them. All the faculty needs a chance to enter into the conversation about the objectives. Inherent in these objectives is the knowledge that good staff development programs may differ in format, but not in substance. Presentation of the theory and demonstration of its use are essential. There must be an intellectual acceptance that it makes sense in a practical way.

Then the professional staff must have time to practice under simulated conditions while receiving structured feedback. Finally, there is coaching for application. Teachers must use the new skill, in the classroom, while being supervised by someone who knows how it should be done. What is learned must be applied.

Keep in mind that the teachers we trust to deal with complicated, volatile, and sensitive issues are sometimes never given the kind of information and feedback needed to gain confidence or experience before facing what amounts to a showdown. All during the last two decades, statistics on teens continued to alarm parents—issues of teen pregnancy, abortion, suicide, drug addiction, or child abuse. In any in-service treatment of such delicate matters, one which could actually help save a student's life, those participating must not simply have the law read to them. For example, imagine that five full days have been set aside to discuss drug addiction and suicide in some depth. Teachers have met with a variety of experts, read excellent papers by leading scholars and have had  time to reflect and question.

One small part of their 'suicide' training is a staged conversation between a teacher and a student.

"How long have you had these feelings, Jim?"

"Long. A few days this time. Most of last summer, I used to sit around figuring out what weapon could kill me fastest."

"But you haven't discussed this with friends? You didn't call anyone to ask for help?"

"Nope. My friends are too busy. They got their own problems and don't want to do anything but party or work."

"But telling me about your feelings, especially about suicide, makes me think that we should try getting someone who knows a lot more than me to possibly help you."

"Like who?"

"Who do you think?"

"I don't know. Not the principal. And not my counselor because all she does is answer the stupid phone when I'm in her office."

"Well, I know sometimes that phone rings a lot. But Mrs. Englert is not always that busy. We could ask her to meet us in an office where we wouldn't be interrupted and explain how we thought it might be best for you to see what she would say about helping out. Maybe give her the chance to do what I'm told she does real well."

"What about my parents?"

"I don't know your folks. I don't know what we should tell them today but they do need to be given the chance to know how you feel."

Agreed, the dialogue may sound tense, guarded, controlled, awkward, or whatever else you can call stilted conversation in some artificial circumstances. But think for a minute about the teacher, a four- or five-year veteran who majored in history and had no psychological training, trying to deal honestly, swiftly, and confidentially with a teenager who has just stopped by to say goodbye because he's planning to take his life.

Practice is needed for such exchanges and the appropriate specialist would, after listening to such a staged rehearsal, be able to tell the staff what the teacher did that was right and what was wrong with the flow of the discourse that could hopefully bring this theoretical student back from the brink of becoming another of those national statistics that shock our country's sensibilities. After receiving structured feedback and solid coaching, teachers will know how to apply what they've learned.

The next step is to make one person responsible for the implementation and assessment of the program. It's interesting that teachers represent 60 percent or more of the total budget, but seldom is there one person's salary allocated for the development needs of the staff. A moderately-sized district with a budget of ten million dollars would spend less than one half of one percent if it allocated one person's salary for staff development.

Let's call this person, who is in charge of a district's staff development, a Staff Development Leader. This person's responsibility would be to search out the best conferences and seminars with respect to the objectives agreed upon. In-service days can then be carefully organized, connected one with the other and structured to instruct, so what was learned would be *applied* in the classroom. The Staff Development

Leader working with competent teachers, could devise mini-courses vis-à-vis the objective during after-school hours.

The focus is on the objective; the focus is on coordinating all of the various approaches: seminars, in-service, mini-courses. The focus is on teachers' learning, changing, growing, and applying what is learned in the classroom.

- **Does your school advance teachers on the salary guide because of degrees or credits accumulated? Were any of the credits collected in one- or two-day 'seminars'? Do you have any evidence that the degrees or credits result in any student growth?**
- **Who goes to conferences? Who chooses the conferences? Are the conferences part of an overall plan to improve student performance in a specific area? If not, why not? Do you have any evidence that what the teacher learns benefits students directly?**
- **Can the school or school district produce their in-service agendas for the past five years? Is it clear what the objectives were? Were the days 'connected'? Was there follow-through on future applications?**
- **Did anything learned in the in-service days help students learn or grow in the classroom? How do you know?**
- **Is a full-time person responsible for staff development? Are conferences, in-service days and mini-courses carefully planned with student needs in mind? How is the staff development program evaluated?**

# Student Feedback

*Is there any mechanism for student feedback to the teacher, especially at the high school level?* In most high schools, students are with the teacher for 45 minutes a day, approximately 180 days each year. Although the student may not always know whether the teacher's knowledge of content is poor, average, good, or outstanding, the students certainly know whether the teacher is warm or callous, accessible or inaccessible, enthusiastic or bored. Of course, many teachers will look at written student feedback as threatening to them, and evaluation by someone without credentials. These concerns are not without merit, but great care can ensure that students do not become the evaluators of teachers. (I am making a distinction between a formal evaluation by a certified administrator-supervisor and communication from students to faculty.)

Notice the rather startling difference between high schools and colleges in this regard. As a high school senior, an eighteen-year-old 'boy' is not allowed to comment on teachers in any formal or informal way. But in January, after the first semester of college ends, the same eighteen-year-old 'man' may actually contribute to the ratings of his college professors.

True, parents seldom live in the same community as their college-age child, and, even if they do, they do not have the same interest in the professor as they did in the biology teacher. Therefore, teachers in a high school assert that a student review may damage their careers, while a student review of a college professor would not.

There certainly are potential problems. But, students have the right under the first amendment to publish *their* review, with or without the support of administrators or teachers. What I am suggesting is that parents, administrators, teachers, and students arrive at characteristics of teachers that students have the maturity and ability to judge. This 'student feedback sheet' can inform teachers and their principal at the culmination of the course.

Will the principal consider meeting with a teacher who constantly received poor comments from students? I hope so! If a number of parents meet with a principal to comment on their perceived shortcomings of a teacher, I hope the principal will check into the situation. A smart principal listens to all sources of information and checks each source out first hand with the teacher if he thinks there appears to be some merit in any contention.

Some teachers will claim that this process will lead to teachers pandering to students in trying to curry their favor. I'm convinced this wouldn't always happen. Students know when teachers have little to say and try to cover it by amusements, jokes, and weak presentation of subject matter. Students may groan and moan about another teacher being hard and demanding. But at the end of the year, if they were asked to evaluate honestly, students will usually have it right on the money. The teacher who is the funny person and told a lot of jokes and took fifteen minutes to get started every day was not respected and admired. The 'hard nose,' the one they said, 'Wanted me to learn, cared about my learning, and was tough but fair,' will receive the respect and positive comments.

An attempt to squash this idea without sitting down to consider its obvious merits is likely. If this happens, I would encourage student councils to devise their own 'Teacher Feedback Form' and implement it in respective schools.

- **Does your high school have any student feedback program?**

# 3
# How to Tell Good Principals from Bad

**"I** think Miss Deborah Apple should be our next principal," said Sandy Bausman. "She has a B.A. from Kenyon and her masters from Harvard. She told us that she initiated cooperative learning and the junior great books program in her last school. That's the type of principal I want; someone who believes in teamwork and cooperation coupled with a solid reading program. And, she seemed to be a very capable person."

"I'll agree she came across well," said Ruth Poteet, "but cooperative learning is the current popular fad in education. Probably, twenty percent of the schools in America have been instituting some type of cooperative learning. So, what does that mean? And the junior great books—possibly a teacher had that idea. Besides, we don't know how well it was implemented or what the results were. I think you are impressed with her résumé and the way she presented herself, Sandy."

"I really resent that, Ruth. If you are so knowledgeable, what have I missed? I didn't see you do anything but follow on my questions."

"Look, Sandy, I don't want to get into an argument with you. I'm not sure what to ask, but I have the feeling that we really don't know who Deborah Apple is, and this is such a key decision for us."

It sure is an important decision, but what should be asked of a candidate for the principalship of your school? If the candidate was a principal in another district and you visit her former school, what questions do you ask? How do you get to know if that person is right for you?

What makes a good principal? How can you tell a good principal from a mediocre one? If you were part of a group whose responsibility was to draw up a list of questions for the interview of candidates for the middle school principal's job what questions from the following categories would you ask?

1. Budgeting experience and priorities
2. Rapport with parents
3. Teacher involvement
4. Evaluating teaching performance
5. Attitudes on discipline

Those are just some of the areas covered in this chapter. Each is important. But collectively, the regard that a building principal has for these and a few other topics will make the difference between a mediocre administrator and an excellent, well-rounded principal.

How you ask the questions is important. But there is no sense in suggesting that only stiff, wooden questions asked automatically in some rigidly dictated order will gain access to the special mind-set of a new principal. You may pick and choose from among the inquiries I recommend in this chapter. Your own priorities may prompt you to add to the list addressed here.

But, it would not be acceptable for a concerned parent to settle for bland, vague, elusive résumé-type data that tells little about the real person who must stand behind the experiences listed on a page attached to the application for a principal's crucial job. Why? Because the responsibilities of a principal's position are far too crucial to be handed over to someone who only looks good on paper.

Successful principals create orderly environments that support effective instruction. They understand what behavioral and academic discipline mean to be effective. They have a vision of what a good school is and systematically strive to bring that vision to life. School improvement is their constant theme and their primary objective is student academic performance. It is often said that the three most important things in real estate are location, location, and location. The three most important objectives of a top principal are instruction, instruction, and instruction.

The twelve areas in this chapter all have instruction as their common theme. They scrutinize existing practices to ensure that all activities and procedures contribute to the quality and the time available for learning. They make sure teachers have the opportunity to participate actively in this process.

This is what principals ought to do. But often there is great difference between what ought to be and what is.

Too many principals have little vision of what their school could become. Although they are decent people, their days are not organized to make an academic vision come true. Instead, precious time is spent reacting to phone calls, to letters in the 'in' basket, and to drop-in visitors. They may be busy but they are not leading their schools academically. They have no agenda of their own and exist to react to the demands of others. Their objective is to 'keep the ship on an even keel,' which usually means maintaining the status quo.

These principals, concerned with their own survival, adopt the 'Uncle Charlie' approach. An Uncle Charlie principal is a good guy and most people like him. He wants to make sure that everything 'goes right.' Many teachers love him and with good reason. He stays out of their way with respect to tough issues and spends time making sure that the supplies are on time and in sufficient quantity, everything is clean and neat, and teacher requests are responded to quickly. 'I'm here to help you,' he often says to his staff. He immerses himself in detail and paperwork and then complains of all the time he spends in 'administrivia.' He 'supports' his teachers, seldom observes them teaching, and when he does, there are very few critical comments. Of course, there is very little academic improvement made under an Uncle Charlie, but then again, he doesn't intend to take any risks. He wants to survive and be happy.

Now let's look at some of the hard things that an Uncle Charlie won't do but an excellent principal will do.

# Academic Vision

A good principal has a clear academic vision of his school and his priorities are academic ones. He can and will tell you when the courses of study were revised. He can tell you what the results are on the third-grade science test, the fifth-grade social studies test or the results of the midterm exams in Chemistry I, Spanish II or English III.

He knows where the problems are academically and he can tell you what his plans are to resolve those problems. He can tell you what his priorities are for the year and state them in specific, understandable terms. He will tell you what his objectives are and how he plans to hold himself and others accountable for reaching them. He will tell you how he is trying to make sure that generalities are reduced to priorities, objectives, plans of action, and assessment. He doesn't talk in platitudes; he talks in specifics. He knows that school and learning is serious business; he has a plan of his own and does not sit back every day to react to other peoples' agendas.

Now consider how this kind of leader gets things done. I met such a high school principal a while ago, who told me about his concern with the declining number of students who were taking foreign languages at his school. Over a period of ten years, the number of students taking Spanish and French declined from 800 to fewer than 400.

He was concerned because children of other countries learned English and often another foreign language, while most of his students were not studying any foreign language. He wanted his students to learn the language of another country and to study its history and culture.

First, he discussed his rationale for increased foreign language study and his plans to accomplish his objectives with teachers, superintendents, the school board, and the community. After his plan was accepted, two foreign language teachers took early retirement. Enthusiastic replacements were hired. French and Spanish clubs were formed and they had an active itinerary. Foreign businessmen visited the school and invited the clubs to meet with them in their establishments in the late afternoon. Visits to cultural and recreational activities were conducted and a foreign film night was held in the school auditorium once each month.

With the principal's constant prodding, support, and enthusiasm German was added during the third year of his initiative. At the end of all these efforts, he got the response he wanted. His high school foreign language enrollment recently topped 1,000.

Because the principal had an academic vision of what was needed and the ability to plan and the tenacity to stay with his plan throughout the years, students' lives were enriched.

- **Can your principal discuss academic priorities?**
- **Does he have comprehensive plans to see that they are accomplished? Are these stated in specifics with respect to fixed responsibilities, an established calendar, standards to be met and evaluation built in?**

# Discipline

The principal is responsible for student behavior. If discipline is excellent, the kudos go to the principal. If student behavior is negative and discipline lax, the first person to demand answers from is the principal.

I knew a principal who took over a very difficult school in California. When she took over, the school's reputation was bad. One fourth of the students were absent on any given day. Test scores were low and gangs were present in the school. Her first act was to establish her office in a bathroom! By placing herself in one of the worst areas of student discipline, she sent a loud and clear message to faculty and students alike—if discipline did not improve, nothing would improve.

This principal laid down the law. She would not tolerate unruly behavior. She held meetings and stayed visible. She convinced teachers to ask more of students. By tackling the problem of discipline head on, she clearly demonstrated the link between discipline and academic progress.

Most principals don't need to take such drastic action, but the really great principals know that good discipline is necessary for a school if learning is to take place. A good principal knows what it takes to get the disciplinary job done and isn't afraid to do it. Principals can run schools in an orderly fashion and purposeful way without making them seem or feel like prisons. It is the principal's job to make it so.

- **How does your principal rate in this most critical area? If the school system is managed right, the board of education has set the proper disciplinary tone with policies on student expectations and a code of conduct. If this is so, then the building principal has the responsibility of carrying out the policies.**

He must discuss discipline constantly with his teachers and students. Yet I have seen schools where the principal never effectively addresses this problem. On a day-to-day basis teachers must make their own decisions with respect to inappropriate behavior and send students to the principal's office. The weak principal, who has little sense of vision or control, often reacts to disruptive students in his office by asking for more administrative help. If he does not get the extra person to assist, he will tell the teachers, "I tried, but the board and superintendent don't care about us."

When this attitude prevails, it is the game of endless ping-pong. The teachers struggle to maintain an academic climate and send the students to the disciplinarian. Since there is no carefully thought out procedure by the principal, the disciplinarian talks to the student and sends him right back into the classroom where the behavior is repeated again and again. This cannot be stressed too strongly. **Where the climate of the school is lax, look to the principal. Where the halls are disrupted, the cafeteria a mess, look to the principal.** The principal must exercise his authority in this area.

# Time

The principal must organize his day in terms of his priorities and focus on instructional issues. Are the courses of study specific and clear with respect to objectives, standards, and assessment? Is time on academic tasks maximized? Is the writing program working to achieve its goals? Is homework used as an excellent academic challenge rather than punishment? Are thoughtful essay questions given on tests? Is the library used independently by students?

To do all this a principal may have to make unpopular decisions. If this means limiting her observations of students engaged in sports activities, then so be it. Instruction and student learning is the focus! The coach knows more about the veer offense in football or the zone trap defense in basketball than the principal. But the principal is supposed to know more about how to organize and get results that will maximize student learning.

I know a high school principal who spends almost every afternoon observing athletic practices and other extracurricular events. She attends almost every home game, play, or activity involving students. She lets parents know that, 'I'm interested in your children' and her presence confirms that interest.

What parents don't realize is this Uncle Charlie principal spends much of her day doing paperwork and then complaining to anyone who will listen. Yet, the reason for her complaints is her decision to spend many hours each day and evening observing student sporting events, plays, and similar events. While this principal spends hundreds of hours each year in this type of activity, where she has little expertise, she spends almost no time on one of her most important responsibilities: supervising instruction.

This principal has no plans or vision for her school and, therefore, doesn't need to meet with faculty after school. Some teachers love this Uncle Charlie because she stays out of their hair. Others feel she doesn't really get at the gut instructional issues and wish she had more time for planning and implementing projects, but they understand because she is 'so overburdened with paperwork.'

Years ago I remember hearing two veteran teachers discuss just this point when I was still new to the business of education. We were out visiting another school on an evaluation team project and after the day's work was done I found myself alone in the faculty room with these two teachers. Even though I didn't know them, they spoke openly about their disagreement over their principal's performance. The remarks were made in such a way that I assumed they had disagreed before about the very same topic. My novice's ears were extremely interested in what I overheard that day.

"Don't complain to me about how the principal's too busy," said one.

"But he is," griped the other, "He works hard. He's always got things to do."

"But instruction and the supervision of instruction are supposed to get his full attention. That's supposed to be his top priority."

"Easy to say. But a lot of other things have to be taken care of too. There are maintenance problems, parental calls, meetings, schedules, and reports galore."

"I know that as well as you do. But he's got to make the time for the top priorities. The rest is secondary. Instruction is always supposed to get top billing and he doesn't make the time for that."

"Yeah, but most things around here are okay as they are. His door is always open and you can go interrupt him if you want. "

"That's just it. I feel like I am interrupting him if I go in to talk about instruction and the improvement of teaching while he's waiting for me to leave so he can count the lunch money or sign the bus passes."

Keep in mind that this was just the beginning of a conversation that was going to become more and more pointed. But it was clear to me that the principal was well liked by most of the teachers because he usually was busy and didn't engage in close scrutiny of the staff. And it was just as clear that the other teacher felt the principal hid behind the apparent burden of trivial responsibilities so he could avoid the really important and complex ones.

Of course, not all principals are like the one they were discussing. I know one elementary principal who meets with parents from 8:00 A.M. until 8:30 A.M., before school starts. She also meets with parents every day from 4:30 until 5:00 P.M. Between 2:30 and 3:15 P.M., she meets with teacher committees who are actively involved in significant instructional issues. During the school day she observes and confers with teachers. The majority of her time is spent meeting with students and teachers to resolve the day-to-day problems of the school. She does her paperwork between 3:30 and 4:30 P.M. and at home when it is necessary.

This principal has her priorities clearly in mind and her days are organized with respect to the priorities. If a principal does not have his priorities clearly in focus, anything becomes important.

- **How does your principal organize her time?**
- **What are her highest priorities?**
- **Does she do the right things or is she always just 'doing?' Does she react to phone calls, letters and visitors or does she pursue her critical priorities and still respond to calls, letters, and requests for meetings?**

Glance at the graphs on the next page and decide which of the time allotment pies represents the kind of average day you would want your child's principal to have.

# Instructional Time

A good principal protects the school day for teaching and learning. He will argue against 'field trips' that add little to what is needed. He will scrutinize every situation when children are going to have the normal school day interrupted. If a field trip is carefully defined, is absolutely integral to the learning of children, and is going to be assessed, an informed principal will support the teacher. Such a leader does not automatically 'sign off' just to keep everyone happy ('Well, the kids deserve a break from the routine.')

*The best principal will fight against shortening the school day and the school year, no matter what the pressures.* He knows that if education is constant the more time spent in learning, the more students will learn. Therefore, he will speak out forcefully against shortening the school day.

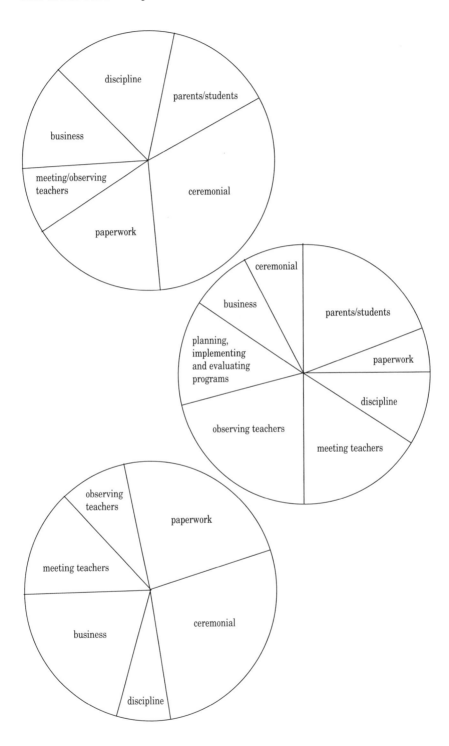

Unfortunately, this does not always happen. I know several principals who were very quiet when students and faculty made an argument to the school board to end the school day at 2:30 rather than 3:15 P.M. "In the fall months, it gets dark at 4:30 and we must leave school at 2:30 in order to play our soccer, field hockey, and football games. We have to miss the last period. If you shorten the day by *only* 45 minutes, we wouldn't have to miss our last period," they argued. And they succeeded with such lame arguments in bringing about an abbreviated school day schedule!

Nonsensically, a school of 1,200 students had the day shortened by almost fifteen percent for the entire year because approximately 100 pupils had to miss one class period twice a week for six weeks. If ever there was a case of the tail wagging the dog, this was it.

Ironically, the principal of this school didn't provide the voice of opposition to this ridiculous proposal when his leadership was most needed. His silence shouted; his wordless message clear. By failing to speak out, the principal showed plainly that he did not value instructional time.

**A top-notch principal will eliminate or curtail the use of the public address system for announcements.** When such interruptions are permitted to distract every teacher and student in a building in order to communicate with one individual who could have been sent a note there is something wrong with priorities. Any such intrusions throughout the school day are symptomatic of indifference to what teachers are doing at special moments in class. Think of how annoying it is for an instructor to be sidetracked after finally reaching that rare moment in a scientific experiment, during the recitation of a great poem, or the emotional center of a discussion of something profoundly important to the personal lives of youngsters who have agreed to give their undivided attention. Only an administrator who had never enjoyed such magically successful moments as a teacher would justify the repeated use of an intercom to call one student to the office while dispelling the attention of the other youngsters in the class.

A good principal understands that a notice can be typed during the late afternoon and read in every homeroom during the first three or four minutes of the next day. During the rest of the school day there should be no announcements on the school address system. If information needs to be conveyed, it can be hand carried by messenger to a particular classroom. The teacher, after considering the message's source, can decide whether to interrupt teaching at that point or relay the message at the end of some segment of the lesson that would provide a more appropriate time to transmit the message.

A former colleague of mine spent a two-month period observing her teachers for the first ten minutes and the last ten minutes of their classes. She then reported to her faculty that it took an average of six minutes before instruction began and instruction ended an average of four minutes before the class bell rung.

Teachers were annoyed she would act in such a 'sneaky' way, and told her so. She listened to their criticism and continued to press her point. "Many of you consistently have students wander in a minute or two late and you wait for them," he observed. "Some of you frequently listen to student excuses why homework wasn't done, which wastes class time; others write what is to be done on the blackboard while the students sit quietly, obviously not engaged in learning." The principal said she would discuss any teacher's particular observations with them privately, although that was not her point.

Her objective was the commonsense notion that the more time spent on learning the more students would learn. The principal discussed the most scholarly research findings which, of course, totally supported this viewpoint. She left the faculty meeting by telling her staff that the ten wasted minutes amounted to 22 percent of the 45 minute class period. She said she was concerned and asked them if they were also.

In the ensuing months, teachers from within the system, as well as a university professor whose special area was academic learning time, made presentations to the faculty. They gave practical suggestions on how to get students involved in learning activities immediately and to keep teaching until dismissal. One teacher coined the phrase 'bell-to-bell teaching.'

Improvement was dramatic. When the principal made her regular observations of teaching three months later, she proudly reported to the faculty that they reduced wasted time to under five percent.

Some faculty became very aware of academic learning time and became 'missionaries' in this regard. They began to work with parents and formed a group they call 'parent assistants.' These parents meet with teachers for one hour each month after school and promise to do drill work at home twice a week for twenty minutes as directed by the teacher.

This principal knew the value of instructional learning time. She made a substantial difference in her school.

- **Does your principal focus on academic learning time? What evidence do you have?**

# Hiring the Faculty

Does the principal of the school have specific criteria when he interviews a prospective teacher? Does he know what is important to him when he interviews? Does the principal actively seek talented teachers or does he simply select from the pool of applicants given to him? Many principals go about the hiring process with an attitude of let's see what applications we have and then schedule interviews. Others have clear and specific criteria against which they screen applicants. If the candidate pool is weak, they actively recruit better candidates. The former approach is lazy and rationalizes mediocre candidates. The latter is assertive and will not settle for mediocrity.

*Does your principal actively recruit teachers? Do you have a brochure telling about your school district so that prospective candidates can know whether they would want to teach in X or Y school district?* If you don't have a brochure which is circulated widely, why not? Do you think that teachers will automatically beat a path to your door? In times when good people are plentiful, this may not seem important. But when the supply of good people diminishes, you will reap the dividends of an assertive approach.

Perhaps four or five districts in a particular area that have the same needs for teachers could hold a recruiting day for prospective teachers in a local hotel. I know principals who do this. The results are unbelievable. For a small cost, these recruiters make the teachers feel that they are something special—which they are. In the morning session the principals tell the teachers why teaching in their specific district is attractive. Depending on the particular district needs and the teachers' qualifications, the afternoon is used exclusively for brief 15- or 20-minute interviews.

In this way principals can interview many candidates for positions they have open. At the same time a prospective teacher can meet with people from more than one district. Not only do the principals screen several candidates, but they leave the impression in many teachers' minds that they are not satisfied with anyone, only the best will do. By their preparation, care, and commitment, they say teachers are important and they want good teachers to teach in their district.

A principal must have the authority to recommend the teachers in his or her school. But, if she is given this authority she must have a carefully organized approach in order to find out whether the candidate is competent in the subject matter, highly motivated, enthusiastic, and caring.

If the principal has a secure ego, she will make sure that her very best teachers are in on the interview process. These faculty members will see things, in terms of the criteria, that the principal may miss. The hiring of a teacher is not a casual process. A good principal will take this as one of her most serious responsibilities. A poor hire will only cause problems for the principal, the district, and especially for the students. A good hire will result in a tremendous learning experience for the students.

A principal in Colorado told me that he wants to hire teachers who "know their subject matter, are enthusiastic about teaching, will take a highly personal interest in each child, and are interesting people themselves." I told him this sounded great and asked him how he conducts his interview. "Our first interview," he said "is conducted by two or three of our best teachers, a guidance counselor or social worker, and a parent. Their objective is to see if the candidate is enthusiastic about teaching and to judge if they will take real interest in each child. Some questions they ask are very general while others are blunt. For example, we may ask the candidate to describe classroom activities designed to hook students on their subject. We also inquire about staying after school and about how a candidate opens communications with parents."

If a candidate is granted a second interview, the team consists of the principal, subject experts, and a teacher from the first committee. "We are interested in their academic competence. We question hard to determine if the candidate knows what they should. We are also interested in them as human beings and probe their interests thoroughly. We want people of good character, wide interests, and high integrity who will be strong role models," he said.

I asked if this wasn't a rather involved and exhausting procedure. "Not really," he said. "I'm interested in building the concept of community and what better way is there to do it than to involve top-notch faculty and parents? Besides, they have insights that I don't. If I weren't thorough, mistakes would be made," he said, "and it would take fifty times the hours we spend to rectify the situation. We work very hard at our questions. We take the interviewing of candidates very seriously."

- How does your principal go about the process of screening and interviewing prospective teachers? Are teachers involved?
- What is your principal's criteria for screening and hiring?

# New Teacher Orientation

When new teachers come into a school, even if they have taught in another district, they usually need some guidance. They must adapt to a new district, a new school, new colleagues, and certainly students who may be different than those they taught before. If he or she is a beginning teacher, one can just double the concern. Yet, in most schools, there is no planned orientation for teachers. What passes for an orientation is usually a half-day or a one-day meeting with the principal the day before school starts. The result of this approach is an overwhelming barrage of routines, procedures, and lists of do's and don'ts.

What should go into a good new teacher orientation program? First, during the summer, the principal should meet with all the new teachers for one day to explain, in a relaxed atmosphere, some of the basic policy issues of the school. Make available to the teachers written materials dealing with student expectations, discipline policy, courses of study, textbooks, the testing program, and so forth.

Second, at least another full day should be spent right before school starts to let new teachers meet their colleagues. The principal can review issues discussed during the summer. Additionally, the principal may want to talk about routine procedures as well as his specific goals and priorities for the schools and how teacher participation is encouraged.

Third, during the first two months of the school year the finest veteran teachers should be paired with a new teacher and they should meet frequently to get over the small hurdles that only experience provides. The mentor can establish a one-on-one relationship so the new teacher can ask any questions he wants without feeling self-conscious.

Fourth, during the first four or five months of the school year the principal should arrange biweekly meetings for new teachers and colleagues within the school who help the organization run effectively. For example, during the first month, a psychologist and social worker may report on some of the problems within the community that are reflected in student behavior. During the next meeting the psychologist and social worker may talk about the functioning of the child study team and how teachers may ask for child study team involvement when a student seems to have serious problems. At another meeting the guidance counselor may talk about the services that guidance provides, what can be expected of guidance, and what guidance expects of the teacher. At another time the teachers who are working on the course of study revision in science may talk about their particular task and how this will contribute to the school's goals.

Finally, the principal must frequently observe the teacher at work in the classroom to see if any problems are developing that adjustments can remediate before they become major concerns.

A program such as the above says to the teacher: "We are really ready to help you. We care. You are important to the functioning of our school and we want to meet with you in order to make the transition correctly."

At the end of the new teacher orientation, which may last five months or the entire first year, the new teacher should have a chance to provide feedback. They can make comments on items like the ones in the following checklist:

1. Assistance with initial confusion
2. Explanation of routine protocol
3. Availability of printed information about staff duties
4. Pre-school availability of administrators
5. Chances to meet colleagues in a meaningful, professional way
6. Effectiveness of the mentor program
7. Consistency of orientation program meetings

In this way the new teacher orientation program is constantly upgraded based on the feedback of the participants.

- **Does your principal have an orientation program? Does it start before school begins and continue throughout the year? What is discussed?**
- **Are teachers new to the system supervised frequently?**

# Evaluating Teaching Performance

A good principal knows that the observation of teaching is one of his most important responsibilities. Over sixty percent of the budget is for teachers' salaries and benefits. Therefore, it's obvious that systematic observation and evaluation where the majority of resources are spent needs top-priority status. Tragically, many principals do not observe teachers at work with students and those that do may make as few as twenty observations per year. When observation reports are written, they are usually in general terms based on loose criteria, frequently having little to do with what research says about good teaching.

Therefore, it is absolutely incumbent upon principals and the central administration to have criteria for the observation of instruction that is 'state-of-the-art.' If one of the principal's most important jobs is the observation of instruction, the criteria for this observation must be first-rate. For example, if the presentation and care of bulletin boards is rated as important and the depth and breadth of questioning skills of the teacher are not mentioned, students are not served well. If the administration does not know that the care and presentation of bulletin boards has little effect on students' learning while the questioning skills of the teacher are important, that which should be evaluated will receive short shrift.

*A principal must spend at least ten percent of her time during the teaching year in the classroom observing teachers and then meeting with them to discuss what she has seen.* Impossible? In a district where I was superintendent, most of the principals did fewer than twenty teacher observations a year. After we discussed the critical importance of the observation of instruction, every principal was routinely doing 120 observations of instruction each year or more, which included a written statement of what the principal saw and a conference with the teacher. *It was done because it was made a priority. And it took about ten percent of the principals' work-day when school was in session!*

The observation must be clear and direct with respect to the criteria. Strengths and weaknesses must be pointed out. A smart principal praises good teaching and promotes the influence of master teachers. When poor performance is noted, supportive principals list suggestions. If there is not progress on the part of the teacher, the principal must make a recommendation to deny salary advancement.

Weak principals will not challenge weak teachers because the Uncle Charlies of the world want to go along and get along. The weak principal wants 'order' most of all. If he challenges a teacher's performance, 'unrest' will rear its head. The teacher, his union, or his friends may inconvenience the insecure principal.

It's no wonder that some principals do very little observation. 'Why jeopardize my salary advancement by rocking the boat?' Uncle Charlie asks. The result: *abdication of a primary responsibility brings financial reward. By not doing what he should, he keeps everyone happy and ensures his annual raise!*

Therefore, when Uncle Charlie has a poor teacher he will 'work around' that teacher. Parents may complain year after year, but Uncle Charlie will deflect these criticisms and tell parents that "some improvement has been noted . . . we have a plan to help . . . there are some skills that the parent doesn't ever see." The principal would rather meet with parents month after month, year after year rather than doing what he knows he should do—confront the teacher.

I cannot stress the importance of supervision and observation of instruction enough. The board of education and the central office may have their priorities in order and the budget may reflect those priorities. District-wide curriculum committees may function and teachers may be involved in responsible professional activities. The courses of study may be excellent with respect to the objectives, standards, and the assessment. However, **the rubber hits the road in the classroom and the only way that we will know that the teacher is effective is to observe instruction frequently with respect to criteria that define excellent teaching.**

A principal I met in Indiana recently put the matter in focus. She claims that "an experienced principal who has carefully trained in supervision skills will know whenever a teacher is doing a capable job. It makes no sense to believe that a weak teacher can suddenly turn it on when an observer enters the classroom and rise to give some great performance on command. It doesn't work that way. A lazy teacher who rises to the occasion when being observed obviously has the ability to do excellent work. For some reason, that person has chosen not to perform on a consistent basis."

This individual is a seasoned administrator who has probably observed hundreds of teachers over a two-decade career. She continued by saying that "the teacher who has the ability and can demonstrate it presents a situation quite different from someone who is struggling. It becomes pretty apparent when a teacher's planning is weak or when tests are nothing more than last minute thoughts to fill up time at the end of a week. Most experienced principals spot that. Then it's a matter of correcting a lack of enthusiasm and commitment rather than wondering if the teacher is without ability."

Her point was straightforward. Only if the principal devotes significant time to observation will a district learn who is top-notch and who isn't. And, if someone with ability is slipping, a good principal must devote the time to find out why. An observant principal won't take too long to locate and help correct the problem.

Central office personnel must read the majority of the observations that principals make. Only in this way will there be effective checks and balances to see that this all important area of administration is taking place. Too often in school districts, that which is critical is neglected and that which is unimportant is done. If the central office makes the principal's evaluation partly dependent on the quantity and quality of teacher observations it will get done. What gets evaluated gets done!

I mentioned before that Uncle Charlie will allow any person to 'drop in' and talk to him about anything. He'd rather do this than observe teachers. Observation is hard work. It also means he might have to confront poor performance. Dealing with 'drop in' visitors is easy and lets the unknowing visitor get a favorable view of the unfocused administrator. The 'drop in' is impressed: Uncle Charlie is accessible and accommodating. He is in his office doing paperwork and responding to phone calls, and 'he took time from his important duties to speak with me.' Charlie might even say 'I know I ought to be in the classroom more, but I'm so busy with other responsibilities I just don't have the time.'

A typical morning in his confused and unplanned course of business will permit a half dozen interruptions like the following.

*Caller Number One:* "Hello, this is Bob So-'n'-So. I'm glad I caught you now because I wanted to know whether we could talk more about that ref's call at the end of the game the other night. Wasn't that something? I'll bet he never saw the runner on second and . . ."

And Charlie lets the athlete's parent drone on about the consequences of something that might be better discussed with the student's coach.

*Caller Number Two:* "Good morning, sir. We met last month at the bake sale for the cheerleaders. If you've got a few minutes, I can finish what I was telling you about that deal you could get on the uniforms for . . ." So begins the intrusion that ultimately is going to be decided by the athletic director to whom this caller should have been referred by the secretary screening the principal's calls.

*Caller Number Three:* "Charlie! How are you today? My wife and I were driving through today and we figured we'd stop by and take you to lunch in half an hour. What d'you say?"

What a weak-willed bureaucrat says is predictable. Because this habitual availability for all and any caller is part of Uncle Charlie's lifelong reputation, he will comply with such requests and forfeit even more of the time that becomes so precious in the crowded day of a focused and well-organized school leader.

And finally there's *Caller Number Four,* representing the quintessential foolishness of this entire problem: "Hello . . . valued customer. This is the computer recording station tape message forwarding vital information to you this morning about new opportunities that are specifically designed to . . ."

And so our befuddled non-leader sits listening for another thirty seconds to a come-on that includes a free trip to Fiji for anyone willing to waste time on calls dialed by telecommunicators whose canvassing patterns are as random as the routine Uncle Charlie follows day after day in his office. He remains fixed at the phone, mindlessly listening to a machine and epitomizing all that is wrong with an educator without clear priorities.

Tragically, he does this at the expense of clear academic priorities such as the observation of teaching. If principals put the supervision of classroom teaching on their list as the highest priority, it would be done. Obviously, Charlie can be counted on to respond to the immediate, rather than do the important.

- **Does your principal make at least one hundred and twenty observations of instruction each year? If not, what 'reasons' does he offer? If he has assistant principals and supervisors, do they also make over 120 teaching observations each year? If not, why not?**
- **If your state has a denial of salary increment provision, when has the principal used it last?**
- **Does the principal work with and/or challenge weak teachers or 'live with them'?**

# Involvement of Teachers

Principals must involve teachers in areas that affect them professionally. Are teachers asked to participate in the modification and revision of courses of study? Is the assessment program reviewed with teachers and are they asked to determine which assessment items to use while testing the students' understanding in each course of study? Are teachers involved in the selection of textbooks and the supplementary materials or are the materials of learning imposed on them from above? Do teachers have a curriculum or instructional council where academic issues, problems and opportunities are discussed?

A principal does not give away his ultimate decision-making authority, but if he uses a more participatory management style involving the people affected by the decisions he makes, those decisions become more attractive for all involved. The instructional expert is not the principal or the superintendent. The instructional experts are the teachers. The best teachers in the school district must play a major role in the decision-making process concerning curriculum.

Therefore, a building principal should not assume that he is the instructional expert. If he is a high school principal, he probably taught in just one area: math, science, foreign language, social studies, or physical education and, that was probably years ago. The principal's job is to help organize teachers in terms of goals and priorities. His job is to ask the tough questions and see that the process of involvement results in the best answers to those questions. That is the principal's role, and it does not change in the elementary, middle, and junior high schools.

Often enough, many elementary and middle school principals did not do their teaching in the particular schools which they eventually lead. Even if they had, just because they are now principals does not mean that they know more than the teacher about specific instructional areas. The principal's job is to set that clear vision of what the school can become. It is the principal's job to understand the distance between the reality of the present and the stated goals, and to have a plan to close the distance between the goals and the reality.

The selection of textbooks is one area where this hierarchy causes conflict. In this situation, the principal should allow teachers discretion to recommend a text within the context of the course of study. **The principal should form a teachers' committee to establish criteria, bring teachers together and then call in the various salesmen to present their products.** Teachers must have the autonomy to struggle with the issues involved. In this area they are the experts, not the principal.

An Alabama principal told me she had never involved teachers in the selection of textbooks. "The superintendent always had a board of education subcommittee select from the three to five of the most popular national textbooks in each subject area." She remarked to me that "teachers didn't complain and they organized their teaching directly from the textbook."

A new superintendent arrived and told this principal that he wanted teachers more involved in the matters that affected their professional lives. "I was a bit skeptical, to tell the truth," said the principal, "but when I saw teachers working on the courses of study, I became a convert. Before, the teachers complied; now they are enthusiastic." When it came time to select textbooks, the principal easily obtained the superintendent's permission to include teachers. "You should have seen their involvement. They matched the various textbooks to what we wanted to achieve in the course of study. This work showed that while one textbook was clearly superior, there were gaps we needed to fill with other reading materials." This principal remarked to me that "involvement surely has worked for me. I don't know why it took me so long to work this way with teachers."

Consider another area where a principal leads by involving his teaching staff. Let's assume the results of the writing assessment were not good. What are the problems? Where are the weak areas? Where do opportunities lie? Perhaps the principal will select a group of outstanding teachers and work with them to structure critical questions. The principal establishes priorities. The teachers, who have the technical ability, must use their ability to get the answers and resolve the problem.

The principal is the leader. She sets the tone. She is the person who states the objectives and then involves teachers, the instructional experts, in moving through a process that will lead toward decisions.

- **Does your principal involve staff in curriculum issues?**
- **Does she respect the best teachers as instructional experts?**

# Recognition

Are excellent teachers recognized for their extra effort and accomplishment? At present, most are not and mediocrity is rewarded the same as excellence. In fact, serious negative effects can result from the present 'all are equal' approach. Great teachers know their rewards are no different than the teacher who prepares lessons hastily, teaches without inspiration, and leaves as early as permissible. The great teachers see the mediocre ones using the same notes year after year, not participating in student activities, and discouraging parent communication. Yet the recognition and rewards are the same!

It is no wonder that these teachers get discouraged, realizing that the school works to the denominator of mediocrity, rather than the denominator of excellence. Too often, the good teachers leave the profession, stifled by the mediocrity syndrome.

*Good teachers deserve recognition for their performance. The object is to reward outstanding achievement and pull the average up, not to seek mediocrity and pull the excellent down.*

Many administrators, especially Uncle Charlie principals, want to keep their schools as conflict-free as possible. Uncle Charlie sees rewarding and recognizing individuals as potentially divisive and he will have none of that! "How can I make distinctions?' he asks, "I have all great teachers." While he recognizes that all students can't have the lead in the play or be in the National Honor Society, he will not have distinctions made with his staff. He will have a school that grades, sorts, chooses, and recognizes students continuously, but not the faculty. When Uncle Charlie speaks of harmony among staff, that is usually his slick cover for lack of backbone.

Listen, for instance, to this exchange between someone pushing for a recognition program and a principal who doesn't want to support it.

"I know the idea seems fair because you just want to share some credit and give a teacher a pat on the back. But somebody else might think we favored the wrong person."

"Then publicize everything we do in the process of selecting the outstanding staff member and get input from as many parties as possible. Make the process airtight."

"That's easier said than done."

"Just take the time and effort. The end result will justify this as a good effort that brought a lot of credit to those involved with giving the award to the right person."

"But parents might say we just promoted ourselves."

"Some people are always going to see these things cynically. Should that stop us only if it looks as if we're patting our own backs? If you've got a great science teacher at the high school or some elementary teacher really sparking class after class year after year, how long do you think that person can go without getting recognition . . . given generously in public?"

"Well . . . that's true. But not every teacher feels the same. Wouldn't this bother someone doing almost as good a job?"

"Fine then. Let the close runners-up have the inside track for next year or choose some way to include a small cluster of the best every year. Pick excellent teachers from every level.

"I still don't know. . . . Maybe if the school board initiated it. Why don't you speak to Doris DiPalma? You're on good terms with her."

"No. You should initiate it and tell the board you're behind the idea 110 percent."

"Well, I would . . . if they wanted that. Some of them think my other duties come first."

"Maybe you can get both those duties and this proposal joined somehow and turn this into a process that will be of credit to your office as well as to a teacher."

"I'll think about it . . . right now I've got to attend to paperwork."

Every person, to some degree, wants to be recognized. To those who are the embodiment of what great teachers are about, let's say: "We know what you're doing. We respect you and we honor you!" **_Does your school district recognize a great teacher once each year at the local Rotary, Lions, or Kiwanis club?_**

Can your staff be 'differentiated' so that teachers with ideas and the ability to translate ideas into action have that opportunity? Why not have staff leaders, a few great teachers who will work an extended school year?

In this chapter, I have already mentioned that new teachers need mentors for the first few months. Ask only the best teacher to fill this important role. Let's expose our new teachers to our best teachers on a day-to-day basis.

Be careful to watch the Uncle Charlie type of principal. In the name of 'harmony' and 'cooperativeness,' and 'pitting teacher against teacher,' he will work against what I have written. He will not want to participate in an outstanding teacher program. He will not let only the best teachers attend top conferences. In fact, he will 'democratically,' let everyone go 'wherever you think best.' (You can be sure that he will not match the conference to student needs, nor will he follow-up with the teacher after the conference to see if what the teacher gained at the conference should be shared with others.) He will also ask teachers: "Who wants to work a week or two during the summer?" "Everyone who wants to be a mentor can be one," says Charlie. Once again, 'democratic' Charlie has been consistent in his abdication of responsibility, his avoidance of recognizing, and rewarding those who are truly deserving.

- **Do you have an outstanding teacher recognition program?**
- **How are teachers chosen to attend conferences and seminars?**
- **Do outstanding teachers have the opportunity to lead in staff development and curriculum revision?**
- **Are the finest teachers chosen as mentors for new teachers?**

# Workplace Issues

## A QUIET PLACE

*Teachers must have a safe and quiet place where they can work alone, discuss academic issues with colleagues, meet parents, and store papers and materials.* In some school districts teachers do not even have a classroom desk of their own and do not have a file cabinet. If we expect teachers to construct outstanding lesson plans which follow excellent courses of study, then each teacher must have a quiet place to work. Perhaps a large area with movable partitions will allow each teacher privacy, shelf space, a desk, and a file cabinet. If work space in the library is available and important for students, why should we do any less for teachers? If we expect teachers to improve their teaching and assessment, then principals must work to provide the physical setting for them.

## SMALL CONSIDERATIONS

There are many small things that a principal can implement to make sure that teachers have the respect they deserve. Each year before school starts, place the supplies the teacher needs for the first few months in her classroom. Provide appropriate numbers of notebooks, texts, workbooks, supplementary reading, pencils, papers, and similar materials.

There must be an adequate number of computers and copying machines available to teachers. *They must have direct access to these machines or, in the case of routine copying, sorting and collating, have secretarial assistance so that when they make a request, it is handled promptly.*

Teacher lunches is another area worth consideration. Additional supplementary choice for teachers boosts morale and their desires should be catered to. Yes, it might cost a little extra money, but it's certainly worth it. What special types of meals might teachers want? Are there enough teachers who like a good bowl of soup a few times each week? If it takes the cafeteria staff too much time to make the ten or fifteen bowls of soup that the teachers would like, can the principal make an agreement with someone in town to make the soup and bring it to the cafeteria? A very small consideration, sure, but one which says 'We care.'

Teachers need and deserve a clean, attractive place in which to eat and relax. *Does the teachers' lunch room have a rug on the floor? Are there couches and lounge chairs where a teacher can sit comfortably and relax for fifteen or twenty minutes if he or she so chooses?* Is there a large refrigerator in the teachers' room, with adequate freezer space, and microwave ovens so a teacher can take specially prepared food, pop it in the microwave, and have it done in two or three minutes?

All of these considerations will take planning, and some will take extra dollars. If principals understand what a good work environment entails, then it is incumbent upon them to do everything possible to make sure it happens.

- **How does your principal measure up to these workplace issues?**

# Budgeting

An efficient principal needs to learn first-rate budgeting skills. This does not mean to merely add the rate of inflation to each line item. The principal who presents a budget year after year with every line item increased by almost the same percentage is not making hard decisions in terms of his school's needs. He is merely accommodating the staff and pushing decisions up to the central office. The principal's responsibility is to determine, with respect to district and building priorities, exactly what his needs are. If one program shows great promise, then he should argue for additional funds. Conversely, if another approach is not working, to continue to ask for increased funds is reprehensible. The principal's position as a leader demands that he will argue only for those funds that will help students learn best.

- **Does your principal ever recommend cuts? Does he say no to poorly proposed plans or simply 'buck them up' for someone else to refuse? Does he have a strong rationale and plans (including evaluations) for a new program?**

# Parents

Parents have concerns about the school curriculum, teachers, drugs, courses, and other matters. The principal needs to respond to these concerns. It is necessary to schedule time to meet with parents on a one-to-one basis. This time must be structured and not open-ended; otherwise 'meetings' become an excuse for a principal's failure to observe classrooms and conference with teachers. I know principals

who never set appointments. When any parent, or for that matter anyone, drops in, they respond for as long as the visitor wishes to stay. This
'availability' signals a principal who has no real priorities and whose
daily tasks are dependent on who calls or drops in. Sticking to a schedule of appointments does not mean an administrator is too 'unavail-
able.' Instead, it indicates that priorities, plans, and timelines are
important and the principal has a clear focus.

One creative principal I know publishes a *Parents Ask* newsletter
twice a year. This brief, to-the-point publication is the result of meetings he holds during the summer and the first two months of school
with a representative group of parents. When he was an elementary
school principal, his concerns one year were in areas such as the new
'hands on' science program, reading groups, the 'gifted' and 'talented'
program, and teachers providing after school help to students. When he
became a high school principal, the procedure stayed the same—only
the questions changed. Now parents had concerns about drug counseling, the National Honor Society, the new grading system, and the hon-
ors math curriculum.

"At times, the concerns of parents are too complicated for a
response in *Parents Ask*," said this successful principal. "One year parents asked so many questions about the guidance department that I
scheduled a series of three public meetings on the topic 'What Does
the Guidance Department Do?' I got more than I bargained for.
Parents were very suspicious of guidance and more questions were
raised than we answered." He went on to explain: "We had to admit
we had weaknesses we weren't aware of and we didn't communicate
our responsibilities too well. We did an in-depth analysis of what we
ought to be doing and what we were actually doing. The result of
almost six months of work was significant change in our organization
and work responsibilities for the next year. We also wrote a ten-page
brochure for parents, responding to the questions they most often
asked."

Needless to say, I was impressed. A short time later, I made a point
of congratulating that principal in a memo I sent. Part of the communication said:

> that in an age when others seem to have run out of ideas, it's refreshing
> to see you coming up with plans that work and programs that can get
> results. The good publicity generated by your commitment and persis-
> tence deserves to be held up as a model for other schools that have not
> yet come to see how important it is for us all to do such things.

In your pursuit of principals who can bring such evidence of leadership to your town, look for those who are as willing to listen to, meet with and work for parents with concerns like those faced by that school.

- **Does your principal bring together parents and teachers to discuss the school's priorities, the problems it faces, and the actions planned to attack those ills? How does your principal know what troubles parents and questions they need answered?**
- **Is the principal knowledgeable about and forthright with respect to the science, math, social studies, and English programs? Is there discussion with parents about what is done for gifted youngsters or for students who are below grade levels in reading?**

# 4

# How to Tell Good Superintendents from Bad

**"T**he superintendent of schools is the chief executive officer for the school district. It is the superintendent's responsibility to make recommendations regarding policy to local boards of education and to implement board policy." So read the terse statement in the annual board of education flyer.

But what do superintendents do? Are they the persons most intimately concerned with the financial order of the district, or is their primary responsibilities to lead academically? Are they the day-to-day major problem solver or the person who sees that all state and federal requirements are met? The answer is all of the above, and much, much more.

To complicate matters the superintendent reports to a board that often lacks stability. (It's not unusual for a nine-member board to be completely replaced within two or three years.) When such changes occur, they are often accompanied by multiple expectations as to what the superintendent should do or how well he has done it.

This singular position sets the tone for the whole district. If the superintendent and board disagree and contentious meetings are the norm, that district will be in constant turmoil. But, 'harmony' between the board and superintendent may signify a weak executive, a person more concerned with his own survival than with improving the district's performance. Some wimpy executives spend most of their time pandering to the individual concerns of board members to the exclusion of plans and action that will improve student learning.

So, how do you tell the real McCoy from the imposter? Who should you treasure and reward and who should you help to seek another career?

This chapter will examine the position from ten reference points. At its conclusion you will know what it takes to be a top flight superintendent of schools.

The superintendent must work with the board and the community to see that goals established truly represent the wishes of the community. The superintendent of schools must translate broad goals into priorities and then work with others to implement specific programs. He guarantees that objectives are clear, responsibility is fixed, timelines are adhered to and assessment is conducted according to the board directive.

The superintendent must attempt to keep the major focus of the board of education on policy issues that pertain to students. In this regard, he must work to ensure that board meetings do not digress into petty issues which capture time and have no real benefit for students.

A successful superintendent of schools needs unusual qualities. He should work well with various groups in the community: board of education, central office administrators, principals, subject-area department chairpeople, teachers, aides, custodians, and others. *First and foremost, the superintendent of schools must look at every situation, every problem, and every opportunity with one thing in mind: What's best for students?*

Although superintendents are pressured constantly on a multiplicity of issues, they must work only for what is in the best interest of students. Whether or not they succeed is often determined by how steadfast they remain to the welfare of students under their charge.

What makes a good superintendent? What are the character traits that such a person should exhibit? And how are they evidenced in any day-to-day work?

# Wide Reading

Outstanding superintendents should know what is going on in the educational arena. They should read widely and know who the real experts are, what they are saying and how that may be applied to his school district. Good superintendents must read broadly about education practice as well as theory in order to link issues with programs that ultimately serve students better.

And they must read beyond educational journals. Even newspapers and magazines can help the superintendent in his or her work. For example, newspapers and magazines have been consistent in citing studies that reinforce the common wisdom that indiscriminate television watching dulls children's minds. Parents wouldn't think of inviting people with values that are contrary to their own into their house for three hours each day to influence their children. But, that's exactly what they do when they allow their children to watch whatever television they choose. Study after study has shown that most children watch more television during a year than they spend in school on their academic learning.

A well-read superintendent knows that before the advent of television children played outdoors with friends after school and talked with their parents at mealtime. Today many youngsters come home after school to catch their favorite television show, often a soap opera, sitcom, game show, or cartoon. For some children, the television is an electronic babysitter. They are passive, not active, and are already couch potatoes, junior version.

If ambitious superintendents read widely, they will also realize that television watching has an obvious link to health issues. The superintendent will know that studies have linked television viewing to the development of obesity in school-age children. Not only do overweight children tend to watch more television, but children who watch a lot of television are more likely to become obese. Common sense, perhaps, but the savvy superintendent can make linkages between heavy, indiscriminate television watching, poor intellectual development, and poor physical health.

The superintendent understands that research shows time spent reading has a high correlation with children's comprehension and the size of their vocabularies. When the superintendent looks at the research in the area of homework, he learns that it is a powerful tool for intellectual growth and most important for students to have thoughtful homework every night, which is corrected the next day. He concludes that leisure reading and solid homework assignments are most positive, while indiscriminate television watching and snacking on high calorie foods has a negative effect on student learning. Again, one might say that this is common sense; but, if this is so, then why doesn't the superintendent make it his business to get the facts, and take concrete action to persuade parents to change their children's behavior?

The effective superintendent should make parents aware of the negative effects of television and the positive effects of becoming involved with their children during after-school hours. *He or she might write a personal letter to parents asking them to eliminate television Monday through Thursday nights and telling parents the benefits of leisure reading for their children. He or she might encourage parents to buy certain books and magazines, provide a quiet place to study, talk to their son or daughter when they have completed their homework, and check it for accuracy and understanding every night.* Perhaps he will send parents recommended books for summer reading or set up summer reading programs at the school or in co-operation with their local library.

When a superintendent reads widely and wishes to apply what is learned for the benefit of students, he must speak out in a clear and forceful voice. In this example, superintendents cannot determine what will happen in the home, but they can influence it. It is the superintendent's responsibility then to read widely, to listen well and to bring what he has learned to the benefit of the students.

- **How does your superintendent measure up in this area? Does he read widely?**
- **What position and action has the district taken with respect to television and reading?**

# Educational Research

Superintendents of schools are not paid to visit libraries and be researchers. But they should know who the authorities are and who can obtain the best information on any subject.

Recently, a local newspaper mentioned that administrators, teachers, and parents had done 'research' and recommended that class size in their districts be reduced, from the present average of 25 to 17, which was the average of two neighboring communities. The 'research' said that the smaller class sizes were demonstrably better. The teachers claimed that having fewer children would improve their morale and that they could deal with children on a more individual basis. They also claimed there would be fewer disciplinary problems. The parents also bought into this 'research.' It was quite natural for them to believe that a reduction of eight children per class would be most beneficial to their children.

It would be so easy for superintendents faced with these opinions to agree. The argument that quality education always means lower class size is a popular one. A twenty-five-to-one class ratio is certainly better than thirty-to-one, according to this logic, and a twenty-to-one ratio is much better than a twenty-five-to-one class ratio. The ideal, of course, might be a fifteen-to-one class ratio. The cost of reducing class size is enormous, but the children are going to learn so much more. At least that's how we are led to believe things work, according to certain sources.

The only catch is the 'research' base. What does research really say? Is smaller always better? People who have done some of the most definitive research in this area, Herbert Walberg and Edward Hanushek, have shown that there is very little difference in children's learning if the pupil-teacher ratio is reduced from twenty-five to seventeen. If the children are average or above-average students, the teacher will teach the class of twenty-five in almost exactly the same manner as the class of seventeen.

For example, if the teacher spends fifteen minutes of class time in a lecture, that is what the teacher will do in a class of twenty-five or a class of seventeen. If the teacher divides the class into small study groups of five, then there will be three or four groups if the class is seventeen or five groups if the class numbers twenty-five.

The superintendent knows the additional cost per child of a teaching class of seventeen rather than the class of twenty-five are enormous, thirty-two percent more. Should we pay thirty-two percent more in costs when some research shows that the results for students in a class of seventeen are no different than a class of twenty-five? Many superintendents know that the research to support lower class size in all situations is not conclusive and the evidence gathered by individuals such as Walberg and Hanushek presents a strong counter to the accepted wisdom.

Parents and teachers will argue that smaller is always better and present 'evidence' to justify dramatically increased expenditures. The superintendent must know what the evidence really says.

- **What does your superintendent know about research? How does he keep informed?**
- **What is his position about class size?**

# Courage

In the preceding example, I stressed the superintendent's need to be guided by research, not led by pseudo-research or pressure using the cloak of 'research.' Let's assume our superintendent knows the difference and in this case realizes that a reduction in class size from twenty-five to seventeen students will have enormous costs and minimal benefit for students. The question then becomes: Will the superintendent of schools have the courage to present to the community and to the board of education the other side of the argument?

Superintendents with courage will present the evidence. In doing so, they will show that the amount of money saved by not reducing class size from twenty-five to seventeen is enormous.

If taxpayers are squeezed in relation to surrounding communities, the responsible action is to say: 'I don't believe that increasing expenditures by thirty-two percent is the right way to go. The children may get very little for your extra money spent and this expenditure will place you in an even more precarious tax position.'

However, if the tax rate is fair and the school district is doing a good job, then programs that show considerable potential for student growth deserve extra support. The excellent, carefully organized, and promising proposal, mentioned a year ago for gifted and talented students in kindergarten through sixth grade, might finally get needed funds. Instead of reducing class size and spending a tremendous amount of money, a smaller sum spent in this particular area might produce desirable returns.

Perhaps the superintendent and the board of education have been discussing a monetary reward for outstanding teachers and have carefully discussed the benefits of providing paraprofessionals to assist teachers in critical areas which have a positive effect on student learning.

Let's assume in this example that the superintendent of schools has presented counter-arguments to what he feels is extravagant spending to reduce class size. Furthermore, the superintendent does not feel that taxpayers are overburdened financially. Quite the contrary, when a good plan is offered, they usually show a willingness to spend money. The superintendent feels that a plan which has monetary benefits for outstanding teachers, paraprofessionals for each grade, and a gifted and talented program will be of greater value to the community.

For example, let's assume there are fifty-one children and two teachers in the school district's first grade. There would be a similar number of teachers in the second, third, fourth, fifth, and sixth grades. If the class size is reduced to seventeen and each teacher receives a salary of $40,000, then the total teacher cost for the fifty-one children, in each grade, is $120,000. If class size is maintained at twenty-five students with only two teachers, then the difference between two teachers' salaries and a third salary, $40,000, is saved. This is the difference between retaining class size at twenty-five or reducing it to seventeen. The saving would be $240,000 in grades one to six.

Here is where the superintendent offers his approach. "Perhaps we could use the extra $240,000 in the following way. Ten thousand dollars, in each grade, or a total of $60,000 would be used to create the pool of money to reward excellence in teaching; $15,000 per grade for a total of $90,000 would provide each grade with a paraprofessional, and the remaining $90,000 would be used to create a gifted and talented program."

The paraprofessional would immediately correct the homework and inform the teacher of the quality during the first ten minutes of the class. Researchers have stated over and over that homework corrected immediately is a powerful force as an incentive for students. Students will complete homework assigned when they know that it will be corrected quickly and graded. The information that the teachers have within the first ten minutes of class will let them know whether the students have mastered the assignment or not. If not, teachers might want to re-teach some aspects.

Also, the paraprofessional can immediately correct short answer test questions since there is a 'right' answer. This allows the teacher to focus on essay questions which are going to be much more helpful in the students' overall ability to write and express ideas. The result of keeping class size at twenty-five would become clearer to many in the community. It would financially reward excellent teachers, gain the advantage of a paraprofessional for every two teacher, and provide for the much-needed gifted and talented program.

The example of financially rewarding great teachers, hiring paraprofessionals and creating a gifted and talented program is for illustrative purposes only. There are many examples that might have great potential for any particular district, rather than the 'benefits' of the common wisdom. The issue is one of courage, the superintendents risking criticism, for what, in this illustration, would be a difficult position.

In a variation of this scenario, the ultimate test of courage faces a school leader in a district where class size is already at seventeen and the board is already paying $120,000 for every fifty-one students. It would take real guts for a superintendent to say, "We are not using our money effectively by having three teachers teach fifty-one students. If we raise the class size to twenty-five, I do not believe student performance will decrease."

Would many superintendents have the courage to undertake such a plan? Tragically, not many would, even if they knew the research was not clear with respect to the class size of seventeen or a class size of twenty-five. The political risks may indeed be too high, and some districts may want lower class size anyway. 'If it has a reasonable chance of helping my kid I want it,' may be the community opinion. Yet, if you were evaluating the performance of the present superintendent, *you just might want to ask some tough questions about class size to see what your superintendent or potential superintendent really knows about research and what he might recommend.* You could assess his creativeness and courage at the same time.

- **Does your superintendent have convictions? Are they backed up by the best research findings available?**
- **Does he back his convictions with courageous action?**

# Social Issues

When I first began administrative work back in the 1960s, I knew a colleague who was beset by many of the same problems that burdened schools across the country. Despite having lots of other duties, he arranged to have Saturday morning sessions so that single parents and working parents could bring problems about their youngsters to his attention.

I remember my friend telling me that during his opening exchanges with parents he was overwhelmed.

"I was flabbergasted," he confessed. "The difficulties that many single parents face are not ones we speculated about in Education 101 or in Administrative Law during graduate training."

"I know what you mean," I said. And, indeed, my own early experiences were informing me in much the same way as far as dealing with certain problems was concerned.

"I sit listening to these parents," he continued, "and I'm the one getting the education. But it's a practical exposure to real life. Ms. X, for example, wanted to know if I could arrange teachers' schedules so she could meet with them when her workday ended, at 5:00 P.M. Mrs. Y couldn't bring her ten-year-old to our extra music lessons because she has no transportation. And Ms. Z was at her wits' end without baby-sitters for her seven-year-old twins whose abusive father was as much a part of the problem as her inflexible boss who couldn't rearrange her work schedule."

"Sounds a little like trying to juggle a master schedule to accommodate a prima donna on the faculty."

"No, Saul," my friend said, "It's worse."

"How?"

"It's worse because in school at least you have some control over factors related to the ultimate success of your plans. Your own priorities can be rearranged and you can create solutions to problems if they are dealt with imaginatively."

It seemed fair enough for him to claim that. The district where he worked, a relatively small, middle-class New Jersey suburb, was fairly stable. Most attempts to improve school-related programs got favorable coverage in the local press. In comparison to problems faced by superintendents in places like Newark or Philadelphia, the issues he addressed seemed manageable.

"I decided to consider establishing a before-school and after-school program in my own district," he said. "At least we would be making efforts where our counterparts were either doing nothing at all or allowing some of their after school activities to dissolve because kids' parents were unable to rearrange hectic schedules to accommodate important extracurricular opportunities for their youngsters."

When I told my friend of my intent to borrow his model, he warned me that starting would be the hardest part of the whole project.

"I just wanted to beg off," he explained, "after hearing some of these problems. At first it was like Solomon's dilemma. I felt I just couldn't come up with solutions that would be fair or affordable." After three or four sessions, he felt he began to see answers to some of the many problems that earlier meetings defined. He told me that he was glad that he didn't give in to the temptation to see these as parental problems that the schools could ignore because they weren't included as items in his job description.

He went on to explain some other things that happened while he struggled to get solutions to the many problems. He said that after he had talked to community leaders the result was the creation of before- and after-school child-care programs that were high in quality and low in cost. Parents of these children were most grateful. Now they could pursue their careers with a feeling that their children were well cared for between seven o'clock in the morning and the time when school began and after school until the parents picked them up. The school superintendent could have ignored the situation and done nothing. But, sooner or later, the problem would have been brought to his doorstep. Times have changed and he had to adjust to these broader societal shifts.

In this example the superintendent relieved the parents of a great burden. Their anxiety level was reduced and they were pleased that the school understood their problems and played a leadership role in helping them. It was no coincidence that the next school budget passed by an enormous majority. The superintendent's leadership had many consequences. The superintendent, who understood the parents' need and reacted accordingly, was working on several levels. Sensitivity and caring were shown and what was done was best for the parents as well as for the child who was helped. Was it better for the child to be alone in the home from seven to eight A.M. and return to the home with a key on a neck string to watch television and to snack? Or was it better for the student to be in a warm, caring place with other children and adults who provided a safe, nurturing atmosphere? The response also worked pragmatically. When the school sent notes home to the parents asking them to read certain books to their children, to check on their homework, and respond to notes or calls from teachers, the parents would listen as they never had before.

What are some of the other implications for schools when both parents work or many families have only one parent at home? More beds in the nurses' areas to be sure. Working parents can't always come for sick children. Teachers will have to meet with parents from 7:30 to 8:00 A.M. and 7:00 to 9:00 P.M. at certain predictable times during each month. Will this immediately be met with enthusiasm by the teaching staff? Probably not, but the superintendent who understands the social trends will understand, just as some dentists understand. They have to change hours to adapt to changing lifestyles of clients. This may mean the adjustment of teachers' working hours, adjustment to pay, and negotiations with the teachers' union. Whatever it takes, the school must be sensitive to the needs of the community and not resistant to those needs and trends.

A good superintendent anticipates and sets forth plans in an intelligent manner. Otherwise, if he is ignorant or resistant to social issues, they will ultimately be imposed on him by parents and citizens.

- **Is your superintendent aware of the broad issues affecting your schools? Is he always one of the first superintendents in the state to see the implications of social trends on the schools? Does he discuss these in a forthright manner with the board, community, and the staff?**
- **Does he see the implications for your school and have a plan?**

## Vision and Practicality

Napoleon once said that "a leader is a dealer in hope." A superintendent should be that kind of leader. He should have a plan to move from what is to what ought to be. It is not enough to convey that tomorrow will be a better day and to raise people's hopes in this regard. It is the superintendent's job to have a clear plan so that a community's goals for its schools are attainable.

*The superintendent's plan must precisely state objectives and tell where the school or the district is in respect to those objectives.* If the superintendent doesn't have a clear sense of where the school district is now, how will anyone know what it takes to make progress? If he doesn't know with specificity what the objective is, then all roads seem equally inviting, since he has no idea where he is going.

Let's take a specific example. One of Central Township's goals is that "all children write clearly and express their ideas in a coherent manner." What are the standards that will determine "write clearly" and "coherent manner"?

What is the present performance of Central's students? How will the superintendent determine the current writing ability of the students? Will exhibitions be used as part of the present assessment of the students? If so, who will set the criteria? Who will judge, and how will consistency be established between the judges? Will tests be used? If so, will he choose nationally validated test A and not test B? Who is involved in determining what test is used? Will experts help choose the right test? Will students be required to submit a writing sample as part of the test? How will the superintendent present his qualitative judgement with respect to what works well in the classrooms now, as well as that which works badly?

The superintendent ultimately needs to present an ideal writing program to the board of education which he feels will meet the goal of "writing clearly . . . in a coherent manner." For discussion's sake, let's assume that this has been done and that part of the ideal writing program is that every sixth grader correctly uses skills learned in the library. Furthermore, using these skills, the students will write a paper on specific topics in social studies and science by the end of the sixth grade. Standards and criteria are established and these alone will determine the scores of papers. In the tenth grade, every student will write a major research paper on a controversial subject currently debated in our country. Standards of composition and grammar are clearly stated and student papers assessed against them.

In order to reach the objectives of the writing program, adjustments may be needed in each grade level. Responsibility for seeing that this is accomplished must be assigned. The implications for staff development are spelled out. Hiring teachers with strong writing skills is made a prime consideration. If part of the plan is to have students write more at every grade level, the burden on teachers to correct papers needs attention. How can this be addressed?

Will consideration be given to hiring paraprofessionals or lay readers? What are the costs? How will we address and reduce the logistical problems from teacher to teacher as a student goes from one grade to the other or from building to building? Students should have writing folders. But what will they contain?

As our program develops, some students will show exceptional talent. Should we have summer programs to develop this talent? What are the objectives? Who will teach? There are obvious implications for gifted or advanced students with conspicuous writing ability, but what about average students? What can and should be done for these students? What are the costs?

In this example I have tried to show that one of the superintendent's most important jobs is to translate the goals of the community into practical programs to accomplish those goals. Good school leaders need the vision, creativity and pragmatism to see that the noble rhetoric of objectives is translated into practical programs that get results. It is not easy work, but good superintendents get it done, and students benefit.

- **How does your superintendent go about translating vision into reality? Does he understand the difference between doing things himself and getting things done?**
- **Does your Superintendent anticipate and resolve issues or does he only react? Can he see the consequences of an intended action, the problems and the opportunities, and easily deal with them?**
- **What is your writing program like? Can you see a comprehensive written plan that is being implemented?**

# Discipline

In chapter 1, I stressed the importance of discipline in the school setting. If a school district is not consistent in its approach to discipline, very little will happen in the academic areas. Clear expectations with respect to student behavior is needed and the staff, board of education, and community must participate in writing the district code. It is then the superintendent's responsibility to see that a consistent approach to discipline is implemented throughout the district.

If she is to maintain the proper order and tone within the schools, the superintendent needs vigilance and tenacity in this regard. This commitment to the community, the board, the principals, the staff, and the students is ongoing. Good superintendents show this commitment day after day after day. Athletic teams constantly stress fundamentals and basics. That is exactly what the diligent superintendent does in this area—by stressing the basic fundamentals of proper behavior.

I know of one superintendent who had a problem with the cafeteria discipline in the local high school. More food hit the floor or was left on the tables than was placed in the trash cans or eaten. The principal said that he couldn't do much because the teachers didn't want this type of duty. If he put paraprofessionals in the cafeteria, the kids would harass them. "We just can't do any better," he said. "Perhaps, we should hire another custodian so that we could keep the mess contained in the cafeteria and it wouldn't go into the halls."

The superintendent's approach was as follows: She told the principal that custodians were to sweep all garbage left on the tables and the floor into a pile after each lunch period and place it in large bags. After a month they would know the average amount of debris per day left on tables and floors from the students. The principal's task, after the month of collecting garbage, was to reduce the garbage from four bags per day to one bag per day. The superintendent clearly defined the problem of garbage in the cafeteria, its exact amount, and reduction goal of this plan.

The principal got the message that excuses wouldn't do. His job called for making a difference in cafeteria management. Faced with a situation where he couldn't turn away from the problem or make excuses, he got to work. He met with teachers, parent organizations, and students. They made changes in the way the cafeteria lines worked and altered some of the food offerings. Volunteers painted murals on the walls, brought plants into the cafeteria, increased the number of garbage cans dramatically, and even had a contest to paint them attractively.

The principal presented his approach to the board and asked for support. He first explained that many people had worked hard to improve the attractiveness of the cafeteria, the food, and the way the cafeteria functioned. He stressed the positives and arranged for the board to tour the cafeteria when in session. He then asked the board to support him if he kept a student after school for throwing food, leaving food on the table, or dropping it on the floor. He suggested that students detained would sweep and wash the floor, clean windows, and water plants. The board agreed enthusiastically.

The results were dramatic. Although the principal did not reach his goal the first month, he did the second month and he maintained the standard of appearance. The superintendent, by keeping the problem paramount in one of the most difficult areas of the school, convinced the principal that discipline and standards of behavior were very important and worth their mutual attention. As often happens, what gets measured gets done.

A conscientious superintendent should keep at the job of maintaining the proper discipline in all the schools. While each principal is primarily responsible for an individual building, the superintendent reports directly to the board for the overall operation.

- **What is your superintendent's position on discipline? Is he able to separate symptoms from causes? Does he realize that the better the discipline, the more children will have an opportunity to learn, and the worse the discipline, the fewer the opportunities to learn?**

- **What does your middle school and high school cafeteria look like?**

# Challenging the Status Quo

The superintendent of schools should not hesitate to examine the school system critically. Too often, some insecure superintendents would rather look away than challenge a cherished "institution," whether that institution be an individual or a particular program. There are political risks when an institution is challenged and that is why some superintendents of schools would rather go along and get along than confront. They know in their minds, guts, and heart that something should be challenged, but hesitate to do so. 'What the heck!' they wonder, 'I know what would happen if I challenge x or y. I'd probably lose anyway because the opposing forces are too powerful and all it would get me is grief or possibly cost me my job.'

It's hard to measure the 'guts quotient' of any superintendent or superintendent candidate that a community may wish to hire. When established programs or individuals have gained support, they become forces difficult to alter even if they are no longer effective. Yet it is in these situations that the true measure of the superintendent is determined. The gutsy educational leader of the community would say, 'We are not getting results and this program has overstayed its welcome.' *A school leader must have the nerve to eliminate a program or reduce it,* and then transfer money to other programs better leveraged in the interests of students.

A bright superintendent will do her homework carefully because challenged, entrenched interests usually react swiftly. Critical superintendents are often called shortsighted and their proposals attacked word by word, sentence by sentence. Terms like 'penny pincher' or 'malcontent' are used by opponents who suggest reformers are against 'quality education.' Crusading superintendents may be called 'unstable,' 'incapable of leading,' and votes of confidence may be taken against them. Anyone who has ever gone through challenging the status quo knows it is not easy, and superintendents under fire always have to wonder if it is worth the aggravation.

Let me give one specific example where some superintendents of schools look away rather than challenge the status quo. The National Study of School Evaluation publishes a manual called *Evaluative Criteria*. It is used by school personnel and visiting committees of educators in order to evaluate particular schools. Superintendents know about this manual.

School personnel prepare a 'self-study' using the *Evaluative Criteria* as the benchmark by which they measure their own performance. The visiting committee, according to the National Study of School Evaluation, is "to validate the evaluation carried out by the school's staff and to suggest changes to improve the educational program." If they feel the self-study is correct, they endorse the findings of the school's staff. If they find inconsistencies, gaps or information which is not true, they are obligated to write these in their final report.

The process is a sound one and many school districts have profited by the self-study and the visiting committee's report. Yet everything is predicated on the *Evaluative Criteria.* The assumption is that the criteria are the benchmarks against which programs are measured best and most accurately.

If the superintendent wants to go along, he will try and do what the criteria says in order to get a good grade. He can then say, 'Our library is first-class.' But it all depends on the criteria. What if the criteria are flawed? What will the superintendent do then?

Pages 452 to 472 of the evaluative criteria, focus on Media Services (formerly called 'the library'). There are ten major subsections: Major Expectations; Follow-Up to Previous Evaluation; Organization and Management; Media Program; Resources; Media Personnel; Facilities and Equipment; Learning Climate; Evaluation; Judgments and Recommendations.

On page 453, one of the seven 'Major Expectations' listed is that "Students make use of learning media resources and seminars." Although it is a generalized statement, its intent is clear—that students use what is there.

However, the next seventeen pages talk in exquisite detail about the various major subsections. For instance, under 'Organization and Management': "The budget provides for audiovisual materials, computer software, membership in consortia" . . . The following factors receive consideration in the selection of media: "curriculum goals and objectives; characteristics of students served; concern of multicultural/multiracial education; learning styles of students" . . . The following factors receive consideration in the selection of equipment: "energy consumption, durability, portability, warranties" . . . Under 'Media Program': "Provides open access . . . provides for the development of research and reference skills to achieve independence in learning;

provides guidance in the selection and use of the most effective media to meet individual needs and abilities." . . . The Facilities and Equipment subsection is very precise in detailing the Environment. "Space allocations for group viewing and listening; adequate acoustical treatment and telecommunication devices" . . . The equipment subsection evaluates the "number of the following available for the exclusive use of this school: opaque projectors, AM-FM radios, tape duplicators, sound synchronizers, audio mixers, video disc equipment, closed circuit TV, microform, printers etc."

The heart of the evaluation criteria comprises detailed lists of attributes of every possible resource that could be placed in a librarian's dream facility; what constitutes a modern facility, how it is organized, classified, furnished, maintained, and staffed.

It's obvious that if one wants to do well in the evaluation of Learning Media Services, the direction is clear: build and staff the facility according to what will be evaluated. And as in most situations, what gets evaluated will be what gets done.

But, there is no explicit section concerning the most important issue: ***Do students use the library, independently or in groups? Do teachers plan their lessons and their major objectives so that students show the ability to gather, sift and analyze information? Is the library central to their work?*** Do students, by their use of the facilities, learn that issues are often complex and that there are often several sides to issues and not one right answer? Do teachers require major papers of most students and is the library the hub of getting information for these papers? And, what type of measurement will be used to show how frequently and how well children are becoming independent learners?

Unfortunately, the answers to these questions are not in the criteria. The only possible aspect of the twenty-page evaluation that addresses this issue is one question under 'Product/Outcomes Evaluation' that asked to "summarize evidence that students are achieving the major expectations of the program. And since one major expectation is that "students make use of the learning resources and services," one might infer that there is at least one aspect concerned with the issue of student understanding and use of materials. However, this attention fades rather quickly when there are no follow-up questions to specifically determine what "make use" means, quantitatively and qualitatively.

Tragically, the emphasis is on equipment and materials: how things are organized, classified, maintained, and the staffing necessary to keep things in shape and available.

All too often this false god of size and things is dominant. 'More' is always requested and there is always more to request! The focus is always on how far we are from the goals. Plans are then drawn and budget requests made for more books, more periodicals, more media, more TV, more conference rooms, more carts, more everything! The wrong goals are pursued and few of the right questions or issues are ever raised.

The superintendent must have the guts to challenge a system which addresses false goals. Tough questions should aim at real issues. For example, in many elementary schools, children are taught library skills which are seldom used. It's no wonder that these skills need review grade after grade. If a student is taught but what is learned is not applied and reinforced, it quickly becomes forgotten. *The superintendent must see that schools have a library skills program. She should gather evidence that children use the library constantly and that they can independently secure information.*

Do children come to the library individually or in small groups? Are they able to use the library's resources with minimum help from the librarian? Is it normal for children to constantly visit the library to learn from sources other than the text?

Perhaps the superintendent finds out that elementary libraries have class visits on a predictable basis. The librarian reads to students and attempts to interest them in books they may want to read. This is fine as far as it goes, but too often the use of the library ends with class visits. If this is the primary use of the library the superintendent has much work to do with the principals and librarians!

When students reach high school, the superintendent may find that skills have to be re-taught again because few students recall what they 'learned' in grades K–8. Many students in high school may have one assignment per year where the library is used. Most often this assignment has books on 'reserve' that the student must read. If this is the case, an aggressive superintendent needs to alter the patterns of the building principal and librarians.

A major purpose of the library is to make available to all students the wonderful world of information and different viewpoints. When teachers and librarians work together, the student benefits. The child's world is expanded and redefined. The superintendents who take the time to check will see that, tragically, this seldom happens. As a result, most high schools will not see students coming and going to the library in a constant stream, digging out information on their own to supplement class activities.

The library is intended as the intellectual center of the high school. Students should demonstrate their research skills, their independence, and pursuit of truth in the wonderful world of books. Yet, in most cases, this area that has so much to give is underutilized to a shameful extent. *When you visit your school, don't be too easily impressed by the materials in the library. Instead, stand near the library door for half an hour and observe the traffic in and out. Observe too what students do in the library.*

In most high schools, students in the library are there to read a few popular periodicals, have a quiet place to do homework, or perhaps change the scenery from study hall. What the library should be and what it is are often miles apart.

There are always legitimate needs for books, tables, clerks, and the like. Just make sure that the improvement plan for the library doesn't focus on what 'things' we don't have, to the exclusion of questions that focus on students. If you are always led down the path of 'we need more,' then the people who are concerned with 'things' will never be satisfied and the real issues will not surface.

Use the following series of questions as a checklist while reviewing the efficiency and quality of any library program designed to assist students.

- **What skills are taught to children? At what grade level? How do we know they use the skills taught?**
- **Are students constantly streaming toward the library to do their own research? How many children are in the library during the school day? What are the children doing in the library?**
- **Is the library open after school? Is it crowded?**
- **What evidence is there that the library is the learning center of the school?**
- **Is there evidence that the students are becoming independent library users and self-reliant learners?**
- **Does your superintendent challenge and confront the 'logic' of 'we've always done it this way.' What is your superintendent's knowledge of a comprehensive library program?**

# To Listen, Manage, and Inspire

If superintendents hope to lead and manage other people, they must be good listeners. While superintendents are helping students grow, they must listen to many different individuals and groups. The purpose of this section is to give a few examples of how a superintendent may listen to citizens and teachers.

The superintendent should hold well-publicized meetings with parents. Much like the principal, a superintendent makes time when parents are available and this usually means during evening hours or on a Saturday morning. Topics of concern to parents are chosen and announced well in advance. Perhaps local concerns will center on such district issues as the new disciplinary code, the proposed sex education course, or the proposal to change the way teachers are paid. Other issues might pertain to why the busing pattern for the three elementary schools changed. Why was the science program changed in the middle school? What is the effect of the new long range plan for the high school on the tax rate? If the superintendent feels confident that he knows specifics, he might choose to meet with parents and citizens by himself. However, if he feels that he needs expert support, then he should invite professionals from the staff to assist him.

At times the superintendent may wish to have meetings with no prepared subject so that parents can stop by and 'ask the superintendent.' In most cases, a well-informed superintendent will answer such questions immediately. If that's not possible, the thorough administrator will get the facts, phone the parent within forty-eight hours, and answer the question.

A superintendent may meet periodically with a group of 'key communicators.' These are people who are excellent listeners themselves and who have a good feeling for the pulse of the community. The superintendent may meet quarterly with his group and ask: 'What do you feel are the big issues with respect to the schools?' Or he may say: 'I have four or five issues that are very important to me and I'd like to know what the community thinks about them.'

I know a superintendent of schools who has met with a group of about twenty-five key communicators for over a decade. In this town of 20,000, people usually serve for five or more years in this capacity, although there is no commitment for a specific period of service. Presently, one person sits on the town council, another works in the post office, and a third is a barber. The superintendent not only meets with them on a quarterly basis but, at times, calls them personally and asks for their advice. For example, in the local high school a fist fight erupted between two white and two black students. The local newspaper had the headline, RACIAL INCIDENT AT THE HIGH SCHOOL. The story went on in lurid detail. It suggested the fight was a symptom of "deeper problems within the high school" and talked about the administration's failure to address the problems.

The superintendent and the high school principal had worked to improve race relations for years and thought that this was an isolated incident. But what did the people in the community believe? Should the board, the superintendent, and the principal call for an investigation? If they handled it in the normal way, the newspaper might say that was 'proof' that the school really didn't care and was brushing aside a serious problem. Would black parents march on the board and demand that 'racism be addressed'? Would some white parents charge that the school 'was lax and let black kids go unpunished more often than white kids'?

By taking just three hours and contacting twenty of the twenty-five key communicators, the superintendent determined that nobody believed what the paper had said. They knew the positive things going on in the high school and many knew the students involved. They told the superintendent not to worry about the paper. Instead of over-reacting, the superintendent chose a correct course of action because he listened to people who had their fingers on the pulse of the community.

The superintendent must meet with teachers on a regular basis and also meet with faculty when specific incidents require it. If the superintendent involves teachers in major curriculum and policy initiatives, then the teachers know they are involved and valued. If the superintendent in her day-by-day, month-by-month, and year-by-year approach involves teachers, they will know she is not one to pull surprises.

If the superintendent lets teachers know that she will drop by the Lincoln Elementary School next Thursday from 3:00 to 4:00 P.M. or be present at lunch from 12:00 to 1:00 P.M. to meet with teachers, they will respond positively to her. If she says she will listen and she does, teachers will have more confidence in her.

One superintendent I know has a session where building teacher representatives meet with him every other month. The teachers present written questions at that meeting. If a simple question can be answered plainly, it is, and the building representative takes the response back to the faculty. If the superintendent cannot answer the question then and there, an answer is sent back to the building representative within forty-eight hours. The superintendent responds to all of the questions within ten days, in writing, and the answers are circulated in each school. Both the teachers and the superintendent feel that this method of communication makes teachers feel they can get prompt and straight answers to their questions.

Besides being a good listener, a dutiful superintendent of schools strives to become a capable manager. He must have the capacity to define issues, know what needs to change, and what the status is at the present time. This will enable him to move from where things are to where they ought to be. The superintendent must know how to fix responsibility and hold people accountable. An experienced administrator also knows how to delegate and knows that this means not looking over everyone's shoulder on a daily basis. Most superintendents must know that proper budgetary planning is part of their ability to manage well. Timelines must be realistic and respected. *Results* are the 'bottom line.' If a plan is all 'process' and no results, then it isn't much of a plan at all. Yet some superintendents will try to avoid personal accountability. They are long on process, long on resources, long on timelines, but short on results. Good managers do not fear accountability; they manage for results.

The superintendent must be like the short-order cook in the local diner who is able to keep the omelettes, pancakes, sausages, potatoes, and french toast all moving at a rapid pace, although all are at different points of progress. The superintendent must keep track of ten projects at the same time. Each one of these major projects must be well-managed.

When the superintendent says to the board, "You will receive plans for the expansion of Theodore Roosevelt High School in November, the elementary social studies revisions in December, and a report of our drug prevention program's progress in January," the board should be able to count on it.

A superintendent must be able to inspire other people and get them to do more than they thought they could. One such superintendent received complaints from his high school principal and athletic director that there weren't athletic fields available for students after school because of the increased number of women's varsity sports. "We don't have enough fields," the principal stated. "Schedules have to be shortened and students released from class at 1:00 P.M. so we can use certain fields twice before it gets dark in the fall months."

The superintendent and the business administrator met with the principal and athletic director to review this situation. The superintendent knew that a major corporation owned land adjacent to the school's athletic fields. He challenged the principal to work with the business administrator to write a plan that would have the local corporation lease a specific number of acres to the high school for use as athletic fields.

The presentation, he said, would sound something like this: "You are not using the land and we really need it. Lease it to us for one dollar each year. We will transform it to beautiful athletic fields at no cost to you. You'll do a great public service and get plenty of positive publicity. Besides, the kids will play far enough away from the corporate headquarters so they won't disturb anything and it will be attractive to look out the windows to see kids using the fields. We will build an appropriate fence between the athletic fields and your grass to keep stray balls and the like from cluttering your property. If you ever need the land for your own purposes, don't renew the lease."

The principal and business administrator accepted the challenge. They drew an excellent plan, made an outstanding presentation to the corporation and, after months of meetings with lawyers, were able to come to a successful conclusion. The school business administrator, now caught up in the challenge, got the Army Corps of Engineers to work on weekends to level trees and shape the contour of the land in a desirable fashion. The Board of Education, which expected to spend a certain amount of money if the land were obtained, was pleasantly surprised to learn that the project would cost much less than anticipated.

This agreeable exchange occurred on the local level between partners of education and business who realized how much sense it made to cooperate in this fashion. Much larger and more ambitious programs have succeeded as nicely elsewhere across the country over the last decade or so. Major corporations lend their money and administrative skill to dozens of projects that involve state- and federal-level educational personnel. Some of these united efforts were documented and carefully explained by Marsha Levine and Roberta Tractman when they co-edited *American Business and the Public School*. This book presents case studies of corporate involvement in public education.[7] Sections include explanations of how Boeing, Burger King, General Electric, Metropolitan Life, and others have enhanced the quality of schooling for thousands of youngsters, who benefitted by such generosity.

- **How well does your superintendent listen?**
- **Is he a skilled manager who seems to keep many major projects on track effortlessly?**

- **Can he motivate and inspire those he works with to seek imaginative solutions to problems?**
- **Does he see opportunities when others see nothing?**

# Make Routine That Which Can Be Made Routine

Too many people never challenge the big issues because they are forever mired in the routine. They suffer from one of two serious problems. They may not know what is important and they spend all their time in areas that should be reduced to routine procedure. Others know they are avoiding the major issues, but they are content to make big deals out of little procedures. In this way they believe they make themselves less vulnerable. The former is ignorant, the latter is unconscionable. In order to do the important work, immediate routines must be reduced to procedure.

For example, the selection of textbooks is fairly simple. If there is a clear board policy in this area, then the recommended selections are presented to the board in a routine manner.

In the development of a budget, adequate timelines are listed in routine forms developed so the budget process can take place in an orderly fashion. If the left hand doesn't know what the right hand is doing, then arguments and accusations arise. If procedures are clear, the budget is developed with respect to the goals and objectives. Budget presentations are not intended to keep people in the dark, but to say in the most candid manner: 'Here are our priorities. This is the money we need; here is how we are going to measure our progress.'

Assessment of curriculum at all grade levels and subject areas is also essential. This is a process that needs close scrutiny. But once the documents are in place, only routine review and periodic modification are called for. The same is true of course of study revision. If these are changed every five years, there should be a procedure to accomplish this. The superintendent keeps tabs to make sure that the policies are current and the policies are implemented. He does not personally revise the curriculum, but he is responsible to see that it is revised from kindergarten through the high school level.

For reasons treated at length in the chapter on principals, staff recruitment is crucial and it is important to have procedures for the hiring and orientation of new faculty. It is the superintendent's job to see that clear policies and procedures are recommended, implemented, and reviewed as a matter of course.

Staff development is critical for reasons that are obvious to any observer. The superintendent of schools is responsible to see that there is both unity and diversity within the school district. Unity is pivotal for the role it plays in the district objectives of the staff development program. What is learned must be applied. A faculty needs time, whether after school, during school hours or during the summer, to learn new techniques so that students may benefit. The diversity in each school helps to work out the specifics of the program based on the needs of its student body. It is up to the superintendent to make certain that the staff development program is routine in the sense that it is constantly striving to do better in terms of its objectives.

The superintendent is responsible for seeing that outstanding teachers are recognized and rewarded. Here too, certain things are best centralized within the school district. Teacher recognition in one form is a district responsibility. In other areas the recognition and rewards are better determined at the local building level. But it is the superintendent's job to see that the recognition and reward programs are in place and functioning smoothly. He must keep tabs on these at all times and make sure that slippage or neglect does not take place.

Consider the differences, for example, represented by the following two letters. The first, received by a superintendent who failed to realize that some staff expected her to be more concerned than she was with the selection process, is typical of the adversarial mood created when the teacher recognition process goes wrong.

> Dear Superintendent:
>
> We collectively believe that the recent reward given to a valued colleague as Teacher of the Year represents nothing more than the ill-informed opinion of a small number of union members at the high school. There did not seem to be a consensus of opinion among teachers at the elementary level in support of any one candidate. But that should not have permitted a secondary teacher to be chosen for the fifth year in a row and it would seem that this pattern shows that the process is influenced by the number of backers the nominated person can count on for support. If that is the real explanation of how this award is presented, we think the entire program should be eliminated instead of being allowed to frustrate the many outstanding teachers who perform great work in the classrooms but who have no time to campaign on their own behalf for an honor that should be given to the most deserving instead of to the one who is best at self-promotion.

How different a mood is created by this next letter! Contrary to the dissatisfaction expressed by the authors of the first letter, this message is favorable and cites specific reasons why the selection of a competitor seemed fair to the runner up in the district's annual teacher recognition program.

Dear Dr. Wilson,

I wanted to thank you for the advice you gave me confidentially last week at our meeting. As disappointed as I am about not being picked as this year's Outstanding Teacher, nevertheless I know that the program is fair and that the winner was chosen for being able to fulfill her duties in a way that was in fact superior to any other candidate. The whole program made me more aware than I was of just how hard it is to be an outstanding teacher year after year and I feel flattered in some ways that the selection committee thought enough of my nomination to invite me to participate in the final rounds of the evaluations.

Please accept my thanks for the role you played in dealing so prudently with so complicated a process.

Needless to say, parents rarely get to see this side of the inner workings of their children's schools. The men and women who educate youngsters are every bit as proud and sometimes as competitive as the rest of society. Teachers do enjoy the kind of recognition that gratifies their need to be respected and publicly acclaimed for being the best. But the in-fighting and emotional competition that can spoil recognition programs must concern an attentive superintendent, who should be involved with the various stages of the selection process. All proceedings need to be publicized in a timely fashion and any individual worthy of the chance should be given the opportunity to present factual data to a panel without having to launch a campaign that would leave a presidential candidate exhausted.

In the area of business administration, the efficient superintendent must make sure that certain things are routine. Does the school district have a preventive maintenance program? If so, when was it last reviewed? Who is checking to make sure it is implemented? If there is not a preventive maintenance program, why not? Who has the best program around, and can we benchmark it as the basis to develop ours? Are all critical engine parts tagged so we know when to check and grease them? Are the custodians trained to carry out their responsibilities and indicate by their signature that machines have proper maintenance? The superintendent will not answer these questions, but he must see that they are answered. He must make sure that standard procedures become routines accomplished regularly in order to avoid problems.

- **How does your superintendent spend his time? Is he constantly involved with routine affairs that policy and procedures should cover? Take a long hard look at areas that should 'work like a clock.' Do they?**

# Hiring and Evaluating Principals

The research of many prominent educators makes clear the importance of the principal. *If good principals are not hired, the responsibility is the superintendent's.* If good principals are hired, do they continue to perform in an outstanding manner? Does the superintendent set the principal's priorities, are they mutually established, or does the principal set his own?

Many times such priorities are set at such low levels that they are a cinch to accomplish. This is sometimes done because the principal wants to make sure that everything he sets out to do is accomplished. Instead of taking risks in an area that would yield maximum benefits for students, some principals set priorities which are easily achieved and frequently have little to do with the learning of students ('the building will be successfully painted,' 'the principal will conduct a back-to-school night, establish three parental conferences and initiate a fall parent/student picnic,' and so on). Much activity, and the appearance of accomplishment, but direction that completely ignores the rock-hard objectives of student learning and growth.

The principal's major priorities should have one direction—the increased learning of students. A principal's priorities must focus on instruction, instruction, and instruction. This emphasis must be established mutually between the superintendent and principal.

Once established, the superintendent and principal should meet three or four times each year to discuss progress toward the stated objectives. For example, the principal may have the following objectives for the year. 1. Implement a gifted program in grades four through six. 2. Introduce the concept of mastery learning in his school. 3. Demonstrate that the skills taught in the library are actually implemented in the classroom. 4. Raise the math scores twenty percent according to an agreed-upon standardized test. (The prior two years were spent formulating and implementing a better approach to math.)

In each of these areas the principal must have a plan by which he intends to reach a particular objective. The superintendent is primarily interested in the results. In the discussions with the principal, the superintendent may give her advice and counsel if the principal is having a difficult time working through particular problems. But the responsibility to obtain results is clearly the principal's.

At the end of the year the superintendent must write an evaluation of the principal based on his performance. A conference should take place to discuss the evaluation. If there is any dissent from the principal at the end of the conference, the superintendent's evaluation should include it.

Above all, honesty should mark the relationship between the superintendent and the principal with respect to priorities, assessment, and annual evaluation. Clearly understood priorities and objectives highlight a well-written evaluation, one that contains no surprises or hidden agendas.

- **Has your superintendent hired capable principals?**
- **Does she work with principals to establish clear objectives designed to benefit students' growth? Is the progress of a principal's work reviewed with the superintendent at specific times during the year? Is the final evaluation of the principals based upon the priorities and objectives established? Are the superintendent's evaluations of the principals reviewed by the board?**
- **Will the superintendent challenge the principal who is performing poorly?**

# 5

# How to Tell a Good School Board from a School Board You're About to Take Over

**I**magine having the opportunity to sit in the privacy of your own living room for an hour or so with a local board member who willingly revealed answers to the questions you asked. If you had such an unlikely opportunity, you might not even know where to begin your inquiry. Some people would want policies or planning strategies explained. Others might delve into the budget process. Areas like teachers's pay or observation of the board itself might seem taboo. Jockeying for the inside track might create a dialogue as strained as this:

"Could you explain board development plans for the next year or so?" you might begin.

"Not without explaining the state's power to regulate," could be a response.

"Well how about the evaluation of the superintendent?" is a likely second question.

"That would call for an overview of our general approach to assessment," is another evasive reply.

"Well, can we at least treat the possibilities of expanding some extracurricular funds?"

"We'd first have to review the boards regard for the whole budget process."

It's frustrating not to find a suitable point of departure for such an exchange. There are so many facets to board considerations that you might not know where to start questioning a local educational decision-maker.

This chapter addresses the most fundamental areas of board life. There are, no doubt, other aspects to the politics of schools that are important. But after reading the next few pages, you will at least know how to question most decision makers and, by the chapter's end, you'll have a better grasp of the interrelatedness of board business. By then your own questions, like the many I will raise and address, should be clearly focused on the most important fundamentals, the ones that cannot (or should not) be overlooked.

No reader of American newspapers ever has far to look for headlines that grab attention and strive to present education as a controversial and volatile business. And no group involved with the running of our schools is embroiled at the center of educational disputes more often than the local board. A foreigner, glancing at newspaper stories heralded by the following banner announcements, might conclude that America was on the brink of another revolution.

## BOARD OF ED FIRES PRINCIPAL

## UNION BLASTS BOARD

### BOARD TO SUE DEPARTMENT OF ED
### $$$SCANDAL ROCKS BOARD BOAT
### STUDENTS STRIKE TO PROTEST BOARD
### 2 BOARD MEMBERS QUIT IN DISGUST

Such stories begin by prompting readers to think of the politics of education as seething and steamy. In fact, as anyone who's been involved with local policy-making knows, the opposite is more often true. The spectacular or exciting occurs from time to time. But the vast majority of decisions and the routine business of board functioning are low-key operations that have neither flash nor splash. It may be no wonder then that when something out of the ordinary does happen newspaper editors are willing to magnify what may only be a tempest in a teapot.

The reason that boards are regarded by the press as special is because they are the primary policy-making groups in any school district. How well its members work together will say a great deal about the ultimate success of the individual schools.

The main responsibility of a school board is goal setting, policy review, strategic planning, assessment, and reporting on educational quality. It is also important how the board resolves conflict, evaluates the superintendent, establishes teacher pay, and determines budgets. If this represents the majority of your board's decisions, they are on the right track. Disagree with them, if you are so inclined, but know that they are addressing the right issues, not running after topics full of hot air.

# Goals

Goals are broad statements of purpose. At their best, they set the direction of the board of education, the school, the employees, and the community. At their worst, they are hastily-written statements of little practical use.

For example, a school district might have goals such as: a. the ability to write with imagination and clarity; b. the ability to listen attentively; c. the ability to secure and organize information. Another group of goals might be concerned with 'community' and might direct students: a. to understand comparative religions; b. to understand and integrate in daily living the values that our community sees as essential; c. to function productively as a member of a group.

If it takes these issues seriously, the board of education must periodically see that priorities flow from goals. If it doesn't, you know that the establishment of goals was nothing more than an academic exercise.

Goals ought to set direction and establish priorities. If a goal is to have students 'write with imagination and clarity,' then a continuing priority of the board ought to be the writing program throughout the district. What is the ideal sought? What should happen and when? How much will it cost? Who is responsible? How will the board of education evaluate performance? The board's continuing attention to raising tough questions will keep linking goals and priorities.

Another goal statement said that students were to "listen attentively." Many authorities have said that listening skills are very important and our students must be much better listeners. The goal statement acknowledges that and says what should be done, but there is no meat on the bone; there is no action plan to see that the goal is reached. Who are the authorities to guide school employees to help students to become better listeners? Are there any school districts with successful programs that can be replicated?

One school district I know of instituted a year-long eleventh-grade listening and interviewing program that invited local businessmen to classes for questions about career education.

The visitors brought a variety and excitement to the class, sparked interests that were dormant, and made kids sit up and listen carefully. The businessmen talked enthusiastically and specifically about their particular work. They gave examples and asked students for their opinions. Most importantly, teachers felt that students learned how to listen more carefully and how to question people critically.

Some goals may be potential 'hot potatoes.' One goal intended to have students "understand comparative religions." How far does the board wish to go with this? Will the required course in tenth-grade United States history be adequate? The United States history course might briefly discuss 'the cultural differences immigrants brought to the United States.' The course may also make reference to 'an appreciation of the various religions in our country.' Yet, at the classroom level, very little time may actually be spent on the study of comparative religions.

Is this what the board meant? Perhaps not. What the board may have intended was a continuous emphasis from kindergarten to the senior year in the social sciences offerings. The board may have wanted children to read about the major religions of the world in the chronological flow of history. It also may have wanted a full-year elective course in comparative religions at the high-school level.

If this is what they mean, then the approach will be filled with potential problems. Which religions will be studied? Who will determine the reading selections? How will administrators and teachers determine what is appropriate to the learning level of the students? How can the board make sure that teachers are not, unintentionally distorting the beliefs of a particular religion?

It is clear that religion plays a prominent and vital role in American life. On one hand, isn't it questionable for public educators to teach students about economics, politics, or literature in the United States without instructing pupils in the fundamentals of our major religions? But, on the other hand, where is the line drawn on the separation of church and state? Should the schools be allowed to teach anything about religion, even if they try to be objective?

Another goal, "to understand and integrate in daily living the values that our community sees as essential," could also be fraught with problems. What values does the community see as 'essential?' Who will represent the 'community' in arriving at the essential values? For example, if one essential value is 'respect for all people,' this might mean respect for the elderly and handicapped. This value may be integrated into daily living through the high school principal's plan to see that every senior spends at least thirty hours working either in a geriatric section of the hospital or nursing home or visiting patients in institutions for the handicapped.

Even though I mentioned problem areas, this board is focusing on the critical issues and asking the right questions. It is working on its goals, translating them to priorities, and arguing the difficult issues of actual implementation.

Goal statements should be reviewed approximately every five years. There are many ways a community may review and establish goals for their schools. The following is one such approach.

The board may appoint a task force of respected citizens to review and recommend goal statements. They may consider statements from other schools in their state or other states. They may ask for assistance from their state school boards' association or state department of education.

Their recommendations should be widely circulated throughout the community and they should have a series of meetings where residents and task force members can meet to discuss the recommended goals. The task force should report to the board any modifications they wish to make as a result of their town meetings. The board, over a period of two to three months, should hold additional meetings to hear from any citizen who wishes to be on the record with the board vis-à-vis the goal statements. Finally, the board members should discuss the issues publicly among themselves and then vote to establish the community's educational goals.

The purpose of this is twofold. First, the process is thorough and gives the entire community a chance to influence the decision-makers. Second, when a thorough process is used, the community as well as the board of education is apt to use the goals to set policy and priorities.

*If boards choose to act from a basis of goals, policy, and priorities, they are doing what good boards anywhere ought to do. If they do not use goals as the method to direct policy and priorities, then they will be forever reacting to whatever pressure group or fad is currently placed before them.*

Every board of education will spend many hours each month on school business. Are the hours spent in a logical approach that flows from the will of the community as reflected in agreed upon goals?

- **Does your district have goals? Who wrote them?**
- **When were they last reviewed?**
- **Are they used by your board to direct the policy statements, district and school priorities?**

# Policy

The board must also have an established procedure for reviewing its policy statements. If a board does not have an established procedure it is governing by the seat of its pants. A decision made one month may be overturned the next and subsequently changed again three months down the line.

Consider the all-too-familiar action of a 'hypothetical' school board. After considerable debate on the budget, the Bedens City Board decided to save $120,000 and stop 'courtesy busing.' This meant that every elementary child who lived less than one and a half miles from school would have to walk to school, as per state law. Prior to this change, all elementary children were transported as a 'courtesy.'

At the next board meeting twenty angry parents from Montgomery Avenue were letting the board know their feelings. 'Don't you know the speed limit is forty miles per hour on Montgomery, and there are no sidewalks? If any of our children are injured we will hold you morally and legally responsible! That road is hazardous for young children."

After about ten minutes of debate, the board passed a resolution that provided courtesy busing to children in "any 40 mile per hour zone where sidewalks don't exist."

Not surprisingly, at the next board meeting, ten parents from Pleasant Valley Way raised the issue of "a dangerous curve, where Sanford meets Pleasant Valley Way." "Are you telling me," Herb Baum said, "that the curve at Sanford is less dangerous than Montgomery Avenue? You people must be nuts!"

Board members Swayze and Pitney were visibly upset. "Here we try to balance the budget and you get upset because we ask you to train your kids to walk less than a mile to school. We can't please everyone."

After protracted debate the board voted six to three to keep 'hazardous' defined as forty miles per hour and no sidewalks.

Within a month a group called 'Citizens for Safety' formed and ran its own three candidates for the board. The only issue was 'courtesy busing' and Swayze, Pitney, and Beasley, who had voted to end 'courtesy busing' were now soundly defeated.

Because it changed a board policy without public discussion, without understanding the consequences of its action, emotion and anger ruled the day. Several major issues were not addressed, as the whole district became embroiled in a needless controversy.

If the board is a deliberative policy-making body it will not be subject to impulsive change, which is guaranteed to be upsetting to some individuals and groups. Policy must be deliberative and inclusive, not knee-jerk reaction to problems. All policy statements should be reviewed on a predictable basis, perhaps every two or three years. Some states have the requirement that policies must be re-adopted every time a new school board is sworn in, but this becomes very routine because the new school board has no time to thoroughly review forty, fifty, or a hundred policy statements.

If policies have a 'sunset' provision, then the particular policy would be up for review and subsequent elimination, revision, or readoption at a predictable time. The Board of Education would welcome written comments on any particular policy. It would encourage *all* sectors of the community to participate. Written statements on the policy under review would be submitted to the central office, which would organize these and distribute them to the school board. Opportunity to publicly comment on the policy a month or two before adoption will give all community residents the chance to make their views known to the board on a face-to-face basis. This will also allow the board of education to make modifications if it so desires.

Almost all state organizations agree that a local board of education should set policy and see that the schools are run in conformity with that policy. Yet this does not always happen. Instead of seeing to the policy directions of the schools, boards often neglect this important duty and get involved in the day-to-day administrative responsibilities of the schools. Just listen to a typical nonpolicy discussion of The First Winney School District. Topics are discussed, seemingly at random, and decisions made after brief discussion.

"I'm concerned about how the grounds are being maintained at the high school," said Harry Lowery.

"So am I," said Rachel Padilla. "I think we ought to free up some money to kill the dandelions in the spring and give the grass a shot of fertilizer in the fall."

After agreeing to this by a unanimous vote, Ed Snider suggested that a board committee make a decision as to when school might be closed when it snows. "I get a lot of flack on this issue," said Snider.

Harold Reese agreed: "I think a committee is a good idea. Perhaps Ed, Carole, and I could handle that. It would relieve Superintendent Fosdick of that responsibility. He'd probably appreciate that."

Administration is the job of the superintendent of schools, his central office, and the building principals. Once the board has established the policy, it should not attempt to act as the chief school administrator to see that the policy is executed.

- **Does your board of education devote much of its time to policy development and review? If so, is the process open to the public deliberative?**
- **Does the school board understand the difference between seeing that schools are well managed and trying to manage the schools itself?**

# Planning

A board of education should expect that members of its administrative staff be capable managers. Building administrators must master the process of planning. But, if a board of education does not also understand the planning process, it cannot fairly judge the presentations and recommendations of the administration.

Assume the superintendent and members of the staff have worked for six months and are going to present their plan to achieve some goal. If the board of education is not thoroughly familiar with the process of planning, it will not question the school employees thoroughly. Plans that should be rejected, modified, or sent back for further work may slip through because of the board's inability to criticize constructively.

- **Does the board have the ability to define a problem specifically?**
- **Does it know how to write an objective so that it precisely addresses the problem or the intended goal?**
- **Do board members understand what resources are necessary to achieve the objective, and how long the project will take?**
- **Who is specifically responsible to see that the objective is achieved?**
- **How does one consider various options?**
- **How will the board measure its progress in order to know when it has reached its objective?**

Planning is something that people always talk about, but few learn. Yet it is an easily mastered skill. Unfortunately, too many boards of education react to issues in a stimulus-response fashion, voicing their individual bias rather than following a coherent planning process. Decisions made in this manner are often slipshod, causing taxpayers and children problems in the long run.

- **Has your board of education learned how to plan? Does it go about its work in a systematic manner?**
- **Does it evaluate the work of its administration using the same principles of good planning?**

# Conflict Resolution

Conflict in schools will occur on a regular basis. How the board of education handles conflict will determine its effectiveness. If the board of education does not handle conflict well, it will be like a top, spinning aimlessly until it falls totally exhausted with little progress made. In a few weeks or months, conflicts will arise again and poorly informed responses will be given once more.

Conflict may arise suddenly over a book the children are reading. A board of education may be surprised when over one hundred parents attack a teacher, the administration, and the board because of a book that is "suggestive and beneath any basic standard of decency." Parents go on to say, "There is so much good literature and no place for this trash." The teachers' union and other community groups rally to the teachers' defense. "The language may be blunt, but there aren't any concepts that the students haven't discussed before. This is excellent literature and within the teachers judgment and right to academic freedom."

If the board has a carefully-developed policy in this area, they won't have to argue each and every issue from a different frame of reference. Perhaps the policy might state 'appropriate issues for the age group' or that the board wants students to discuss 'difficult social issues, with each side of the issue being discussed' and that 'blunt language may be tolerated if appropriate to the context of the plot.' Furthermore, the citizens challenging the literature would be asked to state exactly what is offensive within the board's policy statement.

If the board of education spends most of its time in policy development and review, debates about such problems as these are solved calmly in the policy development and review process. When the policy is challenged in a volatile atmosphere, the board will know what it did and why it did it. The board can refer to its policy and calmly and thoroughly inform the parents why a particular action or choice was made.

However, even the best boards of education cannot anticipate every situation and have a policy statement to cover it. In order to handle the eruptions that will occur at school board meetings, the board of education must be trained to resolve conflict.

In almost every major city in our country, excellent workshops are given in conflict resolution. Boards of education can learn how to listen, to understand, and to clarify the core issues. They are taught to understand the implications and consequences of each of the positions and shown how to resolve them in a fair and consistent manner.

- **How does your board of education resolve conflict? Do they follow a careful deliberative process or do they make 'seat of the pants' decisions?**
- **When has your board last received training in conflict resolution?**

# Assessment

Another major responsibility of a board is to assess and report on the educational quality of the district. The board of education should have mechanisms in place to measure its long-range goals. For example, if one of the goals is excellence in basic skills, the board should first know how to define 'excellence' and 'basic skills.' Board members should have a variety of measures so that they know where they are with respect to their goal.

The board should establish priorities each year. These priorities are translated by administrative and teaching staff into specific initiatives. These initiatives or plans of action must contain an evaluation of each priority. Within the broad context of goals, the board is setting specific priorities and these priorities are evaluated in the proper way.

For example, an organized, focused board of education will know that in October a progress report is due for the gifted and talented program. In November an evaluation of the compensatory education program is scheduled and in January a report on the grade level tests that were given to first grade through sixth grade students in English, social studies, science, and math will take several hours.

Since the board has done its homework in strategic planning, it knows what the important issues are each month and expects clear and concise reports. The superintendent, central administrative staff, and all employees of the school districts know what the board is about, know its members are thorough, fair, and goal oriented. Therefore, progress reports and evaluation of programs are not only necessary, but expected.

Boards that plan the coming year's schedule carefully project their needs and priorities well ahead of time. Their calendars might look like the chart on the next page. Notice at a glance how much information is readily available and how deliberate the board is in its intended agenda.

When results are excellent, the board should show their appreciation to the school's staff. When results are poor, they should require that the problems be carefully defined and plans made to close the gap between the acceptable level of performance and the present reality.

Other issues may arise during this school year and the board may want reports from their administration in the particular areas. (These may also come at other times in the normal policy review or when a program's performance is reported.) For example, board members may

## November/December: Board Public Sessions

November

| | |
|---|---|
| 2 | Guidance Report on Group Counseling |
| 9 | English Department Recommendation—Writing Program |
| 16 | Elementary Science Program Assessment |

December

| | |
|---|---|
| 7 | Elementary Mathematics—Proposed Changes |
| 14 | Staff Development Program for Next School Year |
| 21 | Plans for Recruiting Staff for Next School Year |

wish to have a report on placement activities of the guidance department. They may spend a meeting or two honing the questions, to make sure that what they are going to ask the administration and the guidance department is carefully done, so they do not waste other people's time. Board members may be concerned with the dropout rate and formulate questions and ask for a report in that particular area.

- **How does your board establish priorities? Are they known to all?**
- **What programs are assessed to see if the priorities are being carried out?**
- **How is the assessment conducted? Are the results presented publicly?**

# Evaluation of the Superintendent

In private or executive sessions, boards of education are able to review personnel matters. It is in these sessions that they should spend time talking about the evaluation of the superintendent. If this is done well, it coincides with the context of a clear job description and yearly expectations.

One of the most important functions any board of education can conduct is the evaluation of its superintendent. It is tragic that many boards of education do not attend to this activity with care. Evaluation is often haphazard and in some instances the board president is simply directed by the rest of the board to 'discuss the superintendent's performance, let her know what type of job we think she is doing.'

The evaluation of the superintendent is critical and should not be a haphazard affair. The superintendent is the chief executive officer of the board and as such should have the opportunity to influence the board, should help the board establish its priorities, and should be the person to implement the board's will. The board can then evaluate performance based on the number of priorities and initiatives undertaken and the difficulty of these priorities and initiatives. The superintendent must reach the standards that the board has set to define acceptable performance. If the board does its work with care, the evaluation of the superintendent, in terms of the board's direction and priorities, is of critical import.

The board of education must carefully review the superintendent's evaluation of principals. The superintendent must evaluate not only the central office, but the building principals who report to him. Too often the superintendent's evaluation of principals is haphazard or, worse yet, nonexistent.

In many districts, principals have formed unions and have organized collectively much like the teachers. They bargain for their salaries on the number of years they have worked and the number of degrees accumulated. At times this salary is indexed against teacher salaries. If a teacher with twenty-five years or more experience and a master's degree plus thirty credits makes $60,000, the high school principal's index might be 1.5 and, with the same credentials and length of service the principal makes $90,000.

*This system is a farce. It rewards degrees, credits, and chronology. It says absolutely nothing about performance. Yet a weak school board will allow this type of situation to go on. It is also convenient for a superintendent since no real evaluation is made and everyone is paid in a clean and antiseptic manner.*

However, the approach is useless because the inefficient and weak are rewarded the same as the efficient and productive. The question is not whether the principals are unionized; the issue is that pay should be based on performance. A board of education should see that principals have a clear job description and yearly evaluations based on clearly defined objectives with specified standards. If the principal's priorities, expectations and yearly evaluations are not performance-based, the board's evaluation of the superintendents should reflect this.

- **Do you know the process your board of education uses to evaluate your superintendent? Is the system performance based, with respect to priorities?**
- **Are the superintendent's evaluations of principals an integral part of the board's evaluation of the superintendent?**

# Teachers' Pay

School boards are ruled by the myth of two C's, chronology (years employed) and course credits. We make the assumption that the older the teacher is, the more experienced and more competent he or she will be. In actuality, *chronology has almost no relationship to teaching proficiency.* A few teachers repeat what they have taught year after year with no modification at all, using the same scribbled notes. Is this experience? Of course not, yet we are slavishly addicted to paying as if seniority equates with excellence.

If the board of education divided the faculty of any school into numbers of years served, the faculty members with twenty-five or more years should be the best, with twenty or more years the next best and those with five years or less the weakest. This, of course, will not be the case. We will find excellent teachers in the least-experienced group, as well as in the more experienced ranges. Whether a teacher is outstanding, merely competent or deficient will have *no relation to the number of years that he or she have served as a teacher.* Yet the myth assumes that we should pay as if experience were the be-all and end-all.

In some states, the pension systems are geared to this myth. In New Jersey, for example, teachers are paid for pension purposes on the average of their last three years of salary. Since chronology (years of experience) dictates that the last three years of salary are the highest, it is no wonder that teachers' unions are consistently arguing for increases at the top three steps in order to give their membership a solid pension position before retirement.

The second C in the way teachers' salaries are determined is course credits. One might say that credit is forever, and be correct. *Although there is no definitive research to prove that taking of disparate courses at the graduate level had any effect on the education that students received, we pay as if it did.* If a teacher takes a course in a particular college, the cost of the course is usually reimbursed. Once sufficient numbers of credits are accumulated, the teacher advances on the salary guide. As mentioned earlier, if a teacher has a bachelor's degree and ten years of experience, he may be paid $40,000. However, if he has a bachelor's plus thirty credits, he will be paid more, perhaps $45,000 a year.

The assumption is that when a teacher takes courses, these courses will result in the teacher's being more effective. Students will then learn more. The trouble with this story is that no proof exists to show it is actually the case. Might not a teacher learn as much in a series of workshops given by independent organizations or the state? If the district has an outstanding staff development program, might not that have a positive affect on the teacher's increased learning?

School boards have paid on *process,* not on *performance.* School boards pay for graduate degrees, disparate courses, and seminars masquerading as courses. Some boards of education have given course credit for travel! Yet, we do not give course credit for other conferences, seminars, or workshops. School boards don't give credit to the teacher who reads widely, learns, and applies the wisdom of the scholars he has read. They pay for means, not ends, pay for attendance and accumulation of credits, not performance in the classroom. Boards have completely missed the point by emphasizing process rather than performance.

What can be done about the situation? The first thing is to recognize it for what it is and to understand that we are paying money that has little relationship to excellence in the classroom. School boards have created and tolerated a system built to false gods. Once they know this, and really make up their minds to improve it, instead of continuing the system year after year after year because 'we've always done it this way,' then boards of education can create a system that is fair.

I believe that good teachers should be well paid. A good starting point is to pay attention to the very first step of the teacher's guide. In states that have organized unions, the union seldom pays attention to the first step because a teacher is not a union member until he or she starts working for the district. Therefore, the teachers' union does not negotiate the first step. This first step, however, is of extreme importance. If the district wants to attract excellent men and women into the profession, it must realize that low salary will only ensure mediocrity.

*What are liberal arts graduates being paid within your school's region? Are you competing for the young men and young women who are thinking about careers in accounting, banking, or sales?* If the beginning salary is not competitive, school boards send a clear message to our high school seniors and to our college freshmen and sophomores who might be contemplating a career in teaching. And that message is: we really do not want the best because we pay so little. So the first step is to make sure the starting salary is competitive.

A rational salary approach, rather than one that rewards chronology and courses, begins by coming to grips with what makes an outstanding teacher. Every school board must state in writing the characteristics and performance indicators of excellent teachers. There is no mystery here—just the willingness to work hard, because the research base is most helpful. The board of education, parents, administrators, and teachers must all be part of this process.

Once this 'hard part' is done, we now have a basis for evaluating our staff in terms of what excellence really is. This, of course, ties in to the necessity of the administration's making frequent observations of teaching instruction. If we don't really know what good teaching is, or if we know what good teaching is but don't observe teachers instructing students, then one system of pay is as good as the next because what we're doing is paying in the dark.

*If school boards really want to have teachers evaluated fairly, they must know what excellence is, commit these statements or indicators to writing, and then make sure their administrators are in the classrooms frequently, assessing teachers in terms of the criteria.* *If school boards do this, they will have the basis for pay based on performance, not pay based on myth.*

There are three aspects of my approach to teacher salary administration. First, an annual raise for all teachers who perform at a level of competence. Second, a procedure to deny yearly raises to staff who do not reach the level of competence. And finally, extraordinary compensation to those teachers who have reached a level of superior teaching in a particular year.

First, if a teacher is doing a good job and meets expectations for teacher competency, he should receive a raise based on the bargaining between the teacher union and management. In states that do not have mandatory negotiations, each teacher who does satisfactory work would qualify for a raise.

Performance then becomes the focal point in a teacher's evaluation. If course work or 'experience' enabled staff to meet the test of competence, so be it. If attending conferences enabled them to succeed, great. If a teacher reads widely and learns from questioning and observing others, that's just fine. The 'bottom line' is competence in the classroom, not 'years served,' 'credits accumulated,' or 'pension aspects' that pump up salaries at the top of teacher salary schedules.

Teachers who do not meet this initial test of competence would have their salaries remain at the same level in the year of evaluation. States that have this provision in law usually call it denial of the salary increment. What this means is the teacher is not allowed to go from Step 10—$45,000 to Step 11—$47,000. The responsibility for improvement is the teacher's, yet the administrators and supervisors also have a responsibility. Their specific criticism should help in suggesting methods for the teacher's improvement.

One might think that management would use the denial of salary increment sensitively, but with sufficient frequency, to make a clear distinction between competent teachers and those who do not deserve a raise. Yet in New Jersey, which has such a provision, less then one quarter of one percent of the teachers, when I was Commissioner of Education, had their salary increment denied! In any organization, more than one quarter of one percent of employees will not meet competency standards. Why then, with such a strong management tool, are only a minuscule number of teachers being graded at less than satisfactory performance?

First, the board of education may lack specific criteria. No teacher should lose any salary advancement because the board and administration have failed to specify criteria. If the board of education hasn't taken the time to have a clear, straightforward and defensible evaluation system, it is in a vulnerable position. Even if there are clear criteria, supervisors should observe teachers frequently. Principals will often shy away from this critical responsibility. They simply do not want to confront the teacher or the union. The result is an abdication of responsibility of the utmost magnitude. The critical observation is avoided and less than competent teachers remain at their posts receiving the automatic salary increase each and every year.

The board of education must make observation of instruction the most important requirement for principals and supervisors. A good board ties its administrators' evaluations to the quality and the quantity of the observations they conduct. Likewise, if nobody is recommended for denial of the salary increment, then the staff may, indeed, be uniformly competent. Much more likely, *if nobody is recommended for denial of the salary increment, a 'live and let live' principal is most likely at work, going along and getting along, working not to rock the boat, rather than keeping students' interests paramount.* States that do not have the denial of increment provision should enact such legislation and those that have such legislation should see that it is not eroded. Otherwise, poor teachers remain forever at their posts.

Tenure laws are very strong and removal is infrequent. New Jersey, for example, has averaged fifteen teachers dismissed through tenure cases involving lack of teaching competence during the period of 1985–1990 and there were 88,000 teachers in the state at that time! It is important, therefore that administration have some control over mediocrity by using denial of increment as a corrective tool.

If we have a fair and clear approach to observing and evaluating teachers and if the board of education demands that administrators emphasize the evaluation of instruction, then it should be easy to distinguish the district's superior teachers from the merely competent.

No artificial quotas should limit the number of teachers in the district who can vie for the outstanding teacher designation. The approach would work like this. Each year the board of education would place a *substantial* amount of money in a pot. For example, let's assume a district with two hundred teachers; the board of education would place $400 for each teacher in this collective pot for a total of $80,000. Assuming that forty teachers met the rigorous requirements for this district's definition of excellence, each teacher will receive a $2,000 bonus for that particular year.

Some teachers or administrators may criticize this kind of program. They will claim it is not possible to differentiate between those who are excellent and those who are merely competent. This is sheer nonsense. In almost every other line of work distinctions are made between those who are competent and those who are excellent. Teachers have no trouble choosing the leads for the play, the solos for the chorus, editor of the yearbook, or inductees to the honor society. Some students are chosen for obvious reasons, while others are not. Distinctions are made and the truly superior receive recognition.

The question of the politics will be justifiably raised. 'If everyone is eligible, you can be darned sure that the majority of teachers will be recommended,' someone will say. 'The principals and supervisors just won't play this game fairly.' They will say, 'almost all of my teachers are great and they should all be considered for merit . . . I can see it now, in our town, the Main Street School will have five merit teachers the first year because Charlie Richmond will ultimately take care of his teachers, no matter what. Here at Queen's Road School, Joan Berriman might not have any merit teachers because she will play it by the book. Then, parents will want to transfer to Main Street because they have the merit teachers, which will cause pressure on Berriman. If she does not recommend merit teachers, her faculty will be up in arms because they will feel they have just as many outstanding teachers as Main street School . . . All you will be doing is building in antagonism between schools and you will see jockeying by the principals to ensure that they have a reasonable quota of merit teachers.'

The board would address this concern in the following manner. After three quarters of the school year has passed, the superintendent would ask the supervisors and principals to share their tentative merit teacher recommendations with central office personnel and other building administrators. Those who were recommended would receive two additional observations: one by a district administrator or supervisor not in their building and one by a respected administrator or supervisor who was not an employee of the district. These observations would be made to confirm or not confirm that the teacher recommended by a principal was truly meritorious. If confirmation were given, that teacher would be recommended for merit. If confirmation were not given, then the superintendent would observe that teacher at least twice and make a determination as to whether that individual would receive merit.

The principal who chooses the easy way out and recommends most of his teachers for merit would be quickly exposed and embarrassed in the light of this process. Since there has been consistent training and the individuals are skilled in writing down what they see, any phony comments and conclusions would be easily flushed out. The pressure brought to bear on a principal who recommends the majority of his faculty, when they do not warrant recommendation, would be swift and sure. If, for example, a principal recommended fifteen out of thirty faculty members and other administrators recommended only three, I do not think that first principal would be recommending so many people the next year, because his ploy would be seen for what is was—a political maneuver so that he did not take any heat for not recommending certain people. (It might also be reflected in *his* salary.)

This is one of the most difficult areas to manage because of human nature and the tendency of some administrators to pass the buck and put the heat on someone else. But, with the safeguard that I have mentioned, a clear check and balance system that others will be reviewing that principal's work, ensures that the 'political' problem can be mitigated to a great degree.

Hard work—sure; plenty of time in the classroom—absolutely. But, it's here in the classroom that learning occurs or doesn't. Our principals and supervisors must recognize excellence and reward it. *They must also confront mediocrity and take appropriate and specific action to see that weaknesses are corrected or that continuously poorly performing teachers are ultimately dismissed from their responsibilities.*

In summation, boards of education must not treat everyone as if they are the same. The outstanding teacher deserves more than the teacher who lacks competency. It's senseless to use a no-fault approach to staff evaluation. As you move to institute a program such as the one that I mentioned, cries of unfairness will arise. Some educators will use anything and everything to perpetuate the 'we're all the same' approach. Don't give in! Focus on distinctions, make the board of education and the administration thorough, fair, and consistent. Don't let them take the easy way out.

Who will speak for the superior teacher? Who will say we recognize what you did for our children this year? Who will challenge the mediocre? The board can, if it is important to them.

Let's reward solid teachers by giving them salary adjustment each and every year. Let's squarely face the teachers who have problems, support them constructively, and show them how to improve. But we cannot look away and deny problems that exist. If troubles persist, deny the salary increment, freeze the salary. If the situation continues, suggest to the teacher that he or she might do better in another profession. And, finally, reward those teachers who are doing an excellent job. Recognize excellence!

- **What is your school board doing? Do you pay for chronology and courses?**
- **Does your school board challenge mediocrity? Do you recognize and reward excellence?**

# The Budget Process

It is also interesting to see how a board behaves during the budget process. If the budget is something that 'has to be done' and has no apparent relationship to what has been going on all year, that will become a major difficulty. Although such proposals are presented with glossy slides, bar graphs, and pie charts, they will essentially show that what was prescribed in the past years will continue to go on, with increases paralleling or exceeding the inflation rate in the specific community.

This line-item budgeting shows that the board of education does not link the budget dollars to the goals, priorities, programs, and assessment, which is its most critical responsibility. If the board did its job all year, it would ask tough questions and get the reports and evaluations on particular programs. Budgets should reflect the direction a board feels is wise with respect to its constant review of policy, priorities, and programs.

For example, let's assume the board expects children to do well in the basic skills and writing is defined as a basic skill of critical importance. If the board believed that writing were central to the development of children in the elementary school, it would approve the superintendent's plan that teachers frequently give essay questions and book reports. Library skills that help writing are ones that teachers could constantly integrate in classes devoted to supporting the board's priority. This board has seen to it that its directive that children write well is carried out in specific action subject to evaluation.

If the results in the writing program are not yet excellent, it should come as no surprise that a writing lab is recommended for the middle school or that college-educated aides are requested in the budget of the high school. The children need to write more and their written work needs quick and careful correction. The budget should then reflect the direction, strength, and performance of the school district.

In order to do this well, there is one more major step that boards seldom take. That is analyzing programs on a cost-per-student basis. It's no wonder that boards don't do this because it is hard work. Most schools' budgets have a line account for 'teacher,' another for 'books,' another for 'equipment.' Each is usually increased every year by a combination of factors—inflation, special interest lobbying and teacher negotiations. The public has no idea how much the English, science, foreign language, drama, or football programs cost on a per-pupil basis.

If line items are re-cast to display the costs for the science teachers, science textbooks, science supplies, and equipment, then the rough cost of the science program becomes clear. When we divide this by the number of students taking science, we have the cost per pupil.

Let's assume the board carefully reviewed science for the past year and decided to add or delete some offerings. The community knows why this is proposed because the board conscientiously worked within the framework of its goals, priorities, programs, and evaluation. Now the board can say, 'By adding the new lab and course in scientific ethics and dropping the course in practical biology the total science program costs look like this . . . '

When you add in all costs and divide by the number of pupils, there is an accurate cost per pupil for any program. Also, you quickly find out that the science program costs more than the English program because scientific equipment has a higher price tag than the books usually required for an English program. The labs cost more and fewer children are in the lab periods. Likewise, the Industrial Arts program costs more than the Science program. Again, this is readily understandable. Fewer students can be safely taught in the Industrial Arts shop. The machines cost thousands of dollars and the depreciated cost on a yearly basis is more than the depreciated cost of the science lab. The cost of the teachers, books, raw materials (wood and metals), and depreciation of the fixed equipment divided by the number of students gives the cost per student here just as it does in the science or English program.

With the football program, we know the cost of the coaches; one must add in the cost of the various uniforms, the first-year depreciation on the fixed equipment that is purchased in a particular year (blocking sleds, weight machines), and the depreciation of machines and equipment already purchased. How much did the new score board cost? Is it used only for football? It depreciates over a ten year period, but if it is used for football and baseball, then perhaps only half of its cost is depreciated for football over the ten-year period. It is not very difficult to come out with a cost per pupil per program even if the accounting of such items is time-consuming.

This approach gives the board of education more knowledge with which to increase, stabilize, or decrease a program. Perhaps a particular program is getting out of hand: the cost is too high relative to the performance of the students in that area. If dramatically increased costs don't bring dramatically increased results, then the board may ask the administration to come up with alternative ways to implement this program. Just because a program costs a lot does not mean the board of education should eliminate it. But the board of education certainly should have the information upon which to make a decision.

Very few boards receive this type of information. Frequently, the administration keeps them in the dark or extols the line item budget. If a board member asks for the cost of a program, an administrator may claim it is 'difficult or time-consuming,' or that it 'increases bureaucratic paperwork.' All too often, busy board members do not have the persistence to demand the information in the form most useful to them.

- **Is there any link between priorities, programs, evaluation, and budget in your district?**
- **Is the normal line item budget re-cast so everyone knows the cost/pupil of each program?**

# Board Development

In their own careers board members see their professional development as being extremely important. They attend workshops and seminars and apply what they have learned to their job. Those who are doctors attend seminars so they can diagnose and prescribe better. Electricians learn about new circuit designs so our homes function better. While professional board members accept career development as an integral part of their 'regular' life, they invariably neglect their development as board members individually and as part of a collective board of education.

Many individual board members have the attitude that they are volunteers and board work is not easy. Going to board meetings three or four times a month is the extent of their volunteerism. "I'll be darned if I'll spend extra time; I'm giving plenty already," one board member recently told me.

I can't quibble that board members work long hours for no pay, but their responsibility is so awesome in terms of dollars and human lives that they must invest in their development. I strongly believe that every board of education should have a policy on 'board development' and the budget needs to show commitment to this matter.

Every year the board of education should spend two to three days in a retreat-type atmosphere. They might review the newest ideas in how to involve the community in goal setting. They might learn more effective ways to conduct policy review and development. They may have experts in conflict resolution review their procedures and work through some realistic issues in this important area. The board may review its approach to strategic planning. Its members should discuss practical problems with a consultant in areas the board needs help on in the next year. This type of approach will sharpen board members' skills and they will face the real issues with greater confidence and ability.

Every organization should invest in itself and I talked often in this book about the necessity for good staff development programs. It is most important that the board of education also step back and examine the most critical aspects of its work two or three days per year. Studying issues such as the ones I've mentioned will bring the board closer together and will give members the skills necessary to do their job in a better manner.

- **Does your board of education take time to 'invest' in itself? Does it have a policy statement on board development?**
- **When did your board last learn together? What areas did they study?**

# Observation of the Board

It is relatively easy to see if a board of education is functioning properly. *By observing the board of education at work over a period of just a few months, you will know whether it is oriented toward goals, policy review, priorities, and carefully drawn plans which include evaluation. You will know by observation whether the board is one that seeks to set the direction, ask the hard questions, evaluate, and report to the public.*

A good board of education talks about the *important* things first, the immediate things second. The weak board reacts to the immediate exclusively, almost never addressing the important issues. **The good board spends at least the first hour of each board meeting discussing policy development and listening to administration and staff reports on progress toward board specified priorities.** The good board's focus is on policy, priorities, and results and they do this first at every meeting.

Wise board members also handle conflict easily and reasonably. They are prepared and trained to listen and to question. They get to the heart of each issue and ultimately decide in an unhurried and fair manner.

I have mentioned what good boards do. At the opposite pole are boards which are enmeshed in the day-to-day smaller problems of the school. For example, a few years ago, one of my assistants observed the performance of the boards of education in four school districts. These were school districts whose performance on state tests and other indicators of school success (attendance, dropout rates, job placement and so forth) was not good. My colleague attended four consecutive board meetings in each district from the beginning to the end of each session. Every fifteen minutes he noted what the board was talking about and then categorized these comments into ten broad areas.

He reported to me that not one board of education talked about goals, priorities, or assessment of programs. Board members talked about students less than two percent of the time over the course of his observations. They talked about such subjects as who would get a particular contract to pave the parking lot. There were constant unfocused arguments between board members and accusations about almost everything, over matters which had little, if anything, to do with the schools' functioning or performance. Political posturing and surprise statements guaranteed to grab headlines were often made. "'board member questions superintendent on petty cash accounts in city high schools . . . cafeteria workers taking home food from refrigerators . . . teachers playing cards in the faculty room."

When I asked to see my assistant's notes in order to check exactly what was said at the intervals when he took verbatim quotes, I was astonished. The words read like the excerpts you would expect to get flipping through a TV dial at a time of day when sitcoms were the only shows available. There was no apparent continuity to the meeting and the snatches of dialogue reaffirmed my deepest suspicions of disorder and turmoil. The lines bounced vacantly off walls in a way that reminded me of a play in which characters didn't even listen to one another.

"I can't understand why the teachers can't control the kids in the hallways."

" . . . but were been over all this before. I still want to know if we are or aren't going to hire a new vice-principal to discipline the kids in the junior high."

"We already know your motives, Harry. You just want to give this job to a person who's contributed to every campaign you've had."

"Well, if we stopped the drug dealers from operating near the schools we wouldn't have so many discipline problems."

"Whatever happened to that program we had set up last year? Didn't anyone follow up to trace its success? How's it doing?"

"We'll have to put that on the next agenda too."

This disjointedness was typical of how imprecise the board was. They handled conflict in the same manner. In a haphazard way, they either agreed or disagreed with each other's remarks. There was little attempt to verify statements. In some cases assumptions were accepted as truth, while in other situations apparently well documented arguments were dismissed. Actions were taken quickly or, just as quickly, serious issues were squashed.

One could make no sense as to the direction of these school districts. Each was like a rowboat filled with nine people who paddled furiously in directions known only to themselves. The boat, at times, was still in the water; at other times it would rush off frantically in one direction; and at still other times move in circles with no apparent rhyme or reason.

- **Monitor what your board of education discusses.**
  **Do they talk about goals, policy development/ review, assessment, budget, or do they just talk aimlessly?**

# 6
# How to Take Control of Your Schools

This book is meant to be a practical manual for change and I have mentioned specifics with respect to what should happen. I have not attempted to write about *how* to change things. What I write in this chapter is an outline of what bases you will have to touch if lasting, positive change is to occur.

## Is It Broke?

Begin with a core group of ten to twelve people who want to see the ideas in this book implemented in your district. Go to the school board, superintendent, principals, and teachers and ask them in a candid but assertive way for information that will enable you to make decisions as to whether your school or district is doing what it should for its students. If you conclude the board of education, superintendent, principals, and teachers measure up, then you have a fine system. Nurture it and give backing in terms of vocal support, as well as resources. The statement 'if it ain't broke, don't fix it' holds true here.

If your analysis and evaluation of your school district shows serious problems, ones that persist, then something needs fixing. Be warned. As Machiavelli wrote in *The Prince,* "There is nothing more difficult to carry out, nor more doubtful of success, nor more dangerous to handle than a new order of things . . . "[8] Any challenged institution or establishment will usually resist change. The status quo will have many defenders, even though its deficiencies are obvious and glaring. It will not change voluntarily because the key players have a lot at stake in continuing things just the way they are. For example, I know one superintendent who keeps the status quo by involving his board in time-consuming, but non-critical, issues. One time he mentioned to me that "the board was getting a little restless, so I presented a report on the possible need for new bleachers on the football field. I formed subcommittees of the board and had manufacturers make presentations. This kept them out of my hair for almost six months."

Let's assume you have taken this book as your guide, measured your district's key players against the questions and found them wanting. What do you do then? While there is not one action that will make everything better, the most important way to begin lasting change is to take control of the board of education. If there are people on the board who are not tied to the present approach, work with them. Meet with them and get their commitment to a bold plan for change.

But, what if the board will not address the issues you have specifically brought to their attention, then what? How do you bring about a change in the board? You are few in number and the system seems supported by many, many old timers. How do you change the composition of the board?

# The Core Group

Let's assume your core group of ten to twelve people has already measured your school district against *How Schools Really Work* and found it wanting. You know where the problems are.

Discuss your total agenda of problems with the core group. Keep at this until you have exhausted yourselves and feel satisfied that you have investigated every aspect of these issues. What problems are district-wide or what issues pertain to a particular school? For example, the grading system in one elementary school is inconsistent between teachers and grade to grade. In another school, homework is seldom given and almost never corrected. The junior high school is noted for an absence of discipline as well as high absenteeism, while the high school guidance program routinely dissatisfies parents. One elementary principal is the personification of Uncle Charlie, going along and getting along, while the high school principal has not confronted a weak teacher in the past five years. Let's assume you have a list of thirty *real* problems—you have the facts.

This is your working agenda. You know what is wrong and you know what you want to do about it. Even before you begin developing your organization, I would caution you not to attempt to change only one or two aspects of your school district. If you do this, nothing much will happen. The system might tolerate the change momentarily and then, month by month, chip away at it until little remains. Initiate a critical balance of change and get it done. In this way you can accomplish lasting improvement.

# Expanding Your Group

Your core group will know many people within the school district whom you might consider for membership in your organization. Though your group will initially attract only parents of school-age children, you may later find community leaders as well as other people who have a stake in good schools.

Expand your core group through face-to-face visits. Have two people visit prospective members in their homes. This is time-consuming, but it will pay off in the long run.

Prompt your core group organizers to see things from the prospective member's point of view. Saul Alinsky, a great organizer and political activist, spoke to this issue when he said that the subjects organizers are presenting "must be immediate enough for a person to care about deeply, specific enough for them to grasp, and winnable enough for them to take the time to get involved."[9] Your core group should consider Alinsky's words very carefully.

I might add one more tip. The school issues should emphasize prospective members' self interest. The phrase, 'What's in it for me?' is a very important one. People will pose this question to themselves even if they don't say it to you.

Before making any home visit, therefore, the core group members must sit down and rehearse exactly what they are going to say when they hope to enlist someone into their organization.

For example, out of your list of thirty critical problems that the schools are not addressing, there might be fifteen 'raw nerve issues' that will be extremely important to your prospective members. Put these issues into groups. Some may cut across all your potential members while others may be appropriate to certain people. You might show that the budgeting process of the school board is a sham and programs are funded because of special interests with no evaluation done on effectiveness. Other issues might be school-specific, appropriate to parents of children who are in those particular schools. Some issues may appeal to senior citizens, while others might be particularly appropriate to parents who wish their children to be admitted to selective colleges.

When core group members visit a home, they must discuss the object of the fledgling organization: 'We intend to make the schools better, to make them more effective and efficient.' The core group members can then use specific examples, carefully researched for their accuracy and appropriateness, to convince the prospective member. The problems must be real, accurately communicated, and understood. An inescapable conclusion will show that your organization intends to help people fight the status quo.

At some point in the home visit, the core group members must seek the commitment of the prospective partner; they must also state that an organization will meet in the next week or two, so that like-minded citizens can come together to do something to improve their schools. Staples[10] says that before the core group team leaves, it should ask the prospective members to write their names, address, and phone numbers. He says that having people write their names makes them feel more committed. Writing their phone number solidifies the commitment and informs the new member that the organization needs their help and will be calling them before the first full meeting.

# The First Meeting

As the core group prepares for the first meeting, it can use a three-stage approach to success. First focus on the problems. If there weren't any problems there would be no solutions necessary or any need for an organization. All of the problems must be stated with clarity and precision. No exhaustive analysis or ten minute explanation of each issues is needed. Be clear and to the point. The whole purpose of airing the problems is to indicate that exhaustive research showed that the schools needed help.

Second, there is a way to improve, and a plan devised, so that things will get better. Here the core committee presents priorities. As I mentioned before, you must work on the whole agenda and not simply nibble at the edges. Yet, you can't do everything at once. Have a sense of those things which are most important to your organization and its membership. Make that feeling clear and plain. The core group's action must be specific, immediate, obtainable. The people who are coming to the meeting to join your organization already understand that the issues you mention are in *their* self-interest. They will have plenty to gain if the priorities are achieved and plenty to lose if the priorities undertaken are not won.

Third, at the first organization meeting, the details of incorporation need attention. Are you a for-profit or a tax-exempt organization? Placing your organization into nonprofit status brings advantages in fund-raising capacity, bulk-mailing privileges, grant eligibility, and so on. Tax-exempt status is even better. It is a little harder to get, but will exempt you from corporate taxes, property taxes, and make you eligible for tax-free donations. (It is always good to have a lawyer or two in your organization so that the incorporation goes smoothly!)

# Planning

Select those in your group who are skilled in planning and let them keep track of everything that is going on. Since you now have a set of priorities, it is time to develop action plans. What are your specific objectives for each priority? Which of your members is most likely to achieve each priority issue? With whom is the responsibility fixed? What tactics are best? Who is in charge of communication? Who will evaluate the success of the particular action?

You have the tremendous advantage of knowing the system is not working well and what needs fixing to make it work better. You know that your target is complete control of the board of education and you are going to keep pressure on through all possible means until you are able to place outstanding people on the board.

Your board of directors, planners, and people in charge of communication will understand that change will not take place with one action. Everyone will not rally to your cause and 'throw the rascals out.' More often, change will only come after a long string of battles that are related. Get set to become totally dedicated and relentless in pursuit of your goals.

As I mentioned, you have a tremendous advantage of knowing about the many problems within the system. You can use a variety of approaches and put the pressure on when you want, thus keeping the opposition guessing about what will come next.

The board of directors, planners, and people in charge of communication must utilize the skills of your total membership. Always make sure that you constantly involve people who want to be involved. Some of your people will be excellent if the tactic used is some form of public protest, while others will be extremely good at letter writing or meeting in small groups with a board member.

A few of your board of directors or people in charge of communication can act as spokespersons for the organization. These people must know the issues inside and out. They are the ones who can present what you want presented in a clear and forthright manner and not get tied in knots by opposition or by the press.

## Confrontation

Wouldn't it be wonderful if the board of education and other employees of the school district, after examining your analysis of the problems and recommended action, say: 'They have certainly made their case and their solutions are what should be done. We are going to stop operating the way we have and turn over a new leaf.'

The chances of that happening are very small. Organizations have evolved over time and have gotten into certain predictable habits. The people in power will want to continue their way of doing things and will probably attempt to dismiss your solutions and your organization in a variety of ways.

Little attention might be given to what you have to say and you may be ignored. Or, the incumbents will form a committee to 'study' what you suggest. The committee will be stacked and take six months to let you know that what you said has little worth. By then, perhaps, some people will not even remember the issue. Alternatively, you may hear that you 'do have some points that may be implemented.' Of course, there is no commitment to implementation, just a desire to dismiss your criticism.

Some defenders of the status quo might attack your organization and describe you as 'crazies,' 'people who do not realize the inherent worth of the school district, people who want to destroy a fine system and people who do not recognize all of the great things that are going on.' Such critics will say that you are wrong on the issues or overly dramatic about some things that are not important. They may cite things they had 'planned' to change anyway. I mentioned some of these tactics because there is little chance that the bureaucracy will agree with you and make changes voluntarily.

In states where teachers are unionized they understand that, at times, conflict and confrontation are necessary to get what they want. Teacher's unions will frequently publicize the unfairness of the board of education and its lack of respect for 'quality education.' They will create conflict over 'low pay, intolerable working conditions, and the failure of the board to involve teachers.' Teachers may engage in nonviolent conflict. One such group stacked their briefcases in the administrator's office at the end of a school day to show that unless things changed, they were not going to take student papers home at night to correct. A 'public vigil' is another example of premeditated confrontation with appropriate signs and press communiques.

Frequently, board members, and administrators will not like such negative publicity with its charges of inadequate working conditions, lack of 'quality education,' and inadequate pay. These are often sufficient to lead the board to cave in and accommodate the teachers' union.

There are many tactics of confrontation you can use to achieve your priorities. In the book, *Parents Unite,* for example, authors Philip and Susan Jones propose threatening an action before you take it.[11] They give an example of a school that is not doing its job. The symptoms are few homework assignments and lax teachers who overlook poor spelling and grammar. Before you take action they suggest confronting the principal with a message like this: 'Mr. Big, we've worked well together on P.T.A. functions for almost three years, but it's clear we've reached an impasse. You say there isn't any problem. We say there is one. You label as inconclusive and meaningless our proof that a problem exists. We met last week to formulate some suggestions for change, and we don't want to see the friendly rapport we've established turn into acrimony. We're not going to take a flat 'no' for an answer. Unless you agree to make some of the changes we've asked for, we're going to do the following: first, we're going to hold you personally responsible if reading scores don't improve by the January test period. We're going to collect papers our children bring home with spelling and grammatical mistakes the teachers don't bother to correct. We're going to tabulate and catalog homework assignments by subject matter to back up our observation that too little emphasis is placed on academic standards.

'We're going to start an information campaign with letters to the editor, the school board members, and to the superintendent, describing exactly what we perceive as the problems you've done little to resolve. We're going to start a petition drive. We believe the results will prove that an overwhelming majority of the other parents share our concerns. We're going to give the editor of the paper our homework tabulations examples of A and B graded papers riddled with spelling and grammatical mistakes. Finally, each one of us is going to write the director of pupil services and request permissive transfers of our children out of this school into other schools in the district.'

The Joneses continue by saying:

> Of course this lets the principal know exactly what you're going to do, and the downside is that he may take immediate action to fight you. He may notify his superiors that a bunch of "crazies" are out to get him. He may tell his faculty that a small group of parents is criticizing and threatening the school. He may also take the offensive and start telling the public how wonderful the school is and how well it's run for children. Yet, if the facts are on your side and you have a strong story to tell, any of his quick attempts to show you as deviants or liars will probably get him into deeper water. Most likely, he will appreciate your telling him about your intentions in private. He just might want to improve, to keep you off his back. If he does this, then you are at least moving things in the right direction. Of course if he's a hopeless case, you have to press for his removal.[11]

Demands and demonstrations are two other types of tactics. Demands must communicate ideas simply and directly. This means the basic idea and not the complexities that stand behind them. Some statements of demands are statements of belief and philosophy such a 'We demand more rigorous academic standards in our schools.' Others are more specific, 'We demand a carefully constructed writing program throughout the grades.'

Focus demonstrations on a single issue and plan them with great care. Appoint someone to deal with the media, and someone else to recruit the demonstration participants or plan for crowd control.

Both demands and demonstrations press the board of education or other 'target' to respond quickly to your particular charge. Yet Robert

Bailey says that 'an effective tactic or protest will not succeed unless three elements are employed; an agenda, public commitment, and a progress report.'

His 'agenda' is the particular demand. Make it specific. The more general it is, the easier it is to circumvent. Holding to your specific agenda will ensure that the board of education will not easily smooth over or deflect the issue. Also, as you prepare the specific agenda you are then forced to reach an agreement on a specific objective you want accomplished.

What you are seeking is a public commitment by the board of education to ensure that it will change a particular condition, program, or policy. This commitment is important because if a board fails to meet its agreement, you can easily go back to your members and recommence the protest efforts. Bailey says that if a commitment is to be effective, the board of education must not only agree to make the change, but must agree at a public meeting.

Bailey's third point is to set a deadline for a progress report. By establishing a deadline and a time to report progress, the board of education agrees to let the public know what it is doing. By consenting to submit a progress report before the deadline, the board agrees to hold themselves accountable to your organization for the completion of the agreed changes.[12]

Staples relates another tactic that you may find particularly appropriate to school boards. He refers to a Ralph Nader strategy which details confronting an institution's own standards. He calls this strategy "by their own petard."

In the example, Nader and his people asked the personnel of an organization about their goals and operating procedures. The institution's personnel talked about how great the place was; they talked about their standards, what they would allow, and what they wouldn't allow. Nader then took their goals and standards and investigated the organization.

He found the stated goals and professed standards stood in stark contrast to what was recorded in his people's observational notes. (He had a group of twenty-five teachers, social planners, and sociologists divided into groups of two and three to carry out three day observational forays into the institution.) His people went to the director's offices, as well as the back rooms. They listened to official explanations and saw day-to-day realities. They spoke with consumers and staff alike. By the time that his people returned from a round of observations, each researcher had brought back between thirty and fifty pages of notes detailing statistical information, conversations, and incidents observed. Included in the raw data, were some *official standards against which they could measure their findings.* Suffice it to say, the reality was much different from the rhetoric of their standards. They were, in fact, hoist by their own petard!

Clearly, the 'by their own petard' strategy of taking the bureaucrats' own standards, makes action research more appealing to the public than other approaches. Staples says: "In adopting the official standards, action researchers give their findings an air of respectability. They align their work with the legitimate authority."[10] At the same time, in accepting or at least giving the appearance of accepting official standards, the researchers seem to be saying that we do not argue with the system's goals. We only argue with their results. The stance immediately places the officials on the defensive. Do they or do they not believe in their own standards? Have they lied to the public? If they have lied, what trust do they deserve in the future?

"Once a single official action is in question," writes Staples, "it becomes more legitimate and less radical for the researchers to ask other questions. Finally, the 'by their own petard' strategy puts officials in the role of deviants by not meeting their own standards they have told the public they should expect. Measured by their own yardstick, officials have but two defenses. They can admit the problem and accept the recommendations or try to discredit the study by personally attacking the researchers while finding fault with some facts to use this as an excuse to question the overall accuracy.' (Since the latter will probably occur, make sure of your evidence and what you decide to make public.)

With some educators, this strategy will work well. When one asks, 'What do you stand for?' the word-bucket will be filled with platitudes and lofty goal statements. Officials will probably state that the welfare of children is absolutely paramount and tell you specifically how they are working to help students. **Then you will check to see if homework is given and corrected. You will check to see if disruptive students are handled firmly without taking time from students who want to learn and teachers who want to teach. You will check carefully to see if parents are encouraged to talk with teachers and how many meetings take place.**

The principal will probably say that the curriculum is well-organized, that the courses of study are constantly reviewed and kept up-to-date. Then, when you investigate, you will find that this isn't the truth: that what was said just does not check out. The principal will probably tell you the physical education program meets students' physical needs and teaches them skills for a lifetime of recreational activities. When you check it, you may find that students could conduct most of the activities themselves while playing pickup games of basketball, softball, touch football, or volleyball. The teacher may not teach skills, but merely supervise the students play.

By checking things out to the last detail, parents can see if the school makes claims it can't substantiate. When this happens, it's relatively easy to hoist some school officials by their own petard.

## Controlling the Issue

In the early months of your group's work, you formed the core, researched the issues and, decided on the total agenda. You built up membership, incorporated, decided on priority issues, and planned your work.

When you 'went public,' you were filled with enthusiasm because you knew that the system you were attacking was a poor one and your solutions would help children immeasurably.

But once your issue becomes public you must control it. This may sound almost self-evident. You may say: 'We know more about the problem than anyone else. How could we fail to control the issue? We worked hard and we know what we are doing!'

What you feel is the issue and what the media says is the issue may differ. Bilken gives an example of an organization established to protect organization rights for disabled children. They worked very, very hard to organize, trained themselves and got ready to go public, saying how they wanted to establish and protect the educational rights of disabled children.

At midday, the parents held a press conference. Their *purpose* was to make their existence as an organization known, to recruit additional parents to their cause and to educate the public to the educational discrimination encountered by disabled children. They wanted to create an image of activism before the public and to stop school district officials from trampling on the rights of disabled children. Simply put, the intended message was 'parent power for children's rights.'

When a reporter asked one parent why the group had gathered, she explained the kinds of problems children with disabilities faced in the public school (exclusion, inaccessible buildings, unnecessary forced segregation from non-disabled children). She spoke expansively of a new parent militancy.

One reporter then asked: "Tell me what it was like to give birth to a disabled child. What were your feelings at the time." Caught off-guard, the parent described her initial guilt feelings of tensions which arose between her and her husband, and of their own depression that the child was not the perfect baby for whom she had planned. The right message was lost!

Bilken continues, "Immediately after the press conference, the parents began to wonder why the reporter had asked the question. Then they worriedly asked themselves, would that highly personal segment appear on the six o'clock news? They could almost predict the answer. The discussion of feelings of guilt, of familial tensions and, of depression fit the all-too-common stereotypical image of the disabled. *It was a story that the media was used to handling,* the kind people take in and let pass with a sigh and perhaps a brief comment, 'Thank God that didn't happen to me,' or, 'Poor woman.'[13]

At six that night when the conference organizers sat down to watch the news what they saw was a woman being asked about her private feelings. The message of rights and of challenging discrimination was lost and never appeared on the television screen. Back in the editing room, the station had put personal human interest before social politics.

Later, it became obvious to core members that they had not controlled the message. They needed to know two things. First, how to say the same thing in at least ten different ways. Second, how to turn any question around so that it could be answered with any one of ten prepared responses. To the reporter's question above, the parent might have answered, 'Oh, I'm so glad you asked that question. Because the truth is that while it took me some time to adjust to the fact that my child was disabled, the greatest problem is the discrimination and neglect he experienced at the hands of our public education system. We pay school taxes like everyone else, yet our child has fewer rights than the other children. We're here today to say our children are having certain rights denied. We intend to correct that.'

# The Media

Your issues are important to you. Present them cogently to make them important to the press. In a nutshell, make your concerns newsworthy.

The press looks for issues that have conflict or controversy, that are understood simply and recognized quickly by many of their readers or viewers.

Your group should define its issue with clarity, otherwise the media or the opposition may define it for you. It is well worth your time to have numerous meetings to define your objectives, so when your spokesperson goes before the camera or microphones, the group's message can plainly be explained.

Communicate what you want to say in a single, simple focus. Most reporters aren't interested in the complexity of your ideas. As mentioned before you must have at least ten different ways of communicating your single core message. Your organizers should develop key phrases and anecdotes to clarify what you want expressed.

You may have a tremendous ally in the local newspaper. More often than not, I have found most local editors interested in good schools and willing to listen to any individuals or organizations that have ideas how to improve them. Visit your editor. Let her know who you are, what you stand for and what you are trying to accomplish.

Remember, editors and reporters like controversy. It sells papers. Your clear presentations of the district's inadequacies and ideas for improvements will gain interest and ink. When an issue is of great import, meet with the editor, explain your viewpoint, and ask for favorable comment on the editorial page.

Letters to the editor help mold opinion. When your supporters submit hundreds of individually written letters, editors will print some. Other people will learn of your ideas and commitment through such letters and will join your cause.

Your chances of getting letters to the editor published are better if they are properly signed, short (one hundred words is a rule of thumb) and worded so that they do not become quickly dated. Try to compose them so that an editor is able to include the letter in any issue during the next month. Be sure the letter doesn't contain any statements that may become inaccurate or misleading twenty minutes after you mail it.

Sentences should be short and punchy if you're sounding off. Lists of statistics don't improve your chances any more than accusations that may allow someone to sue the newspaper. Include your name and phone number in your cover note. Journalists don't have time to correspond for any reason, but someone will almost certainly call you and verify authorship before considering publication. Be available and cooperative, but don't hesitate to ask if any part of the letter is being deleted for reasons of space limitations.

Whether you choose to use the tactics of demands, demonstrations, or try to hoist the board by their own petard, you will need to have clearly written press releases. Reporters refer to basic information as the five 'W's'—who, what, when, why, and where? Your press release must touch these points and should have short paragraphs—ideally no longer than a few lines each.

Sometimes press releases go completely unread because they are delivered incorrectly to offices flooded with vast numbers of similar pages. These may be shuffled quickly by compilers who are interested only in the names and dates of events that are distilled into columns listing upcoming events. If your press release is to be effective, keep the following in mind.

Timing is perhaps the most important element of all. If you call the editor in chief who is coordinating deadlines for twenty articles going to press that afternoon, you'll have no more chance of a decent exchange than you would by reaching an air traffic controller guiding four jets into a single airport.

Drop a note first. Ask for the managing editor when you call ahead of the time when your news is about to become timely. See if it's opportune to speak with someone or stop by to discuss a piece about your group's agenda. Such a visit may help if the part-time writers, called stringers, are too busy or unable to handle education stories. Then deliver the press release that you have prepared. The type of personal connection you have established will make it much more likely for your information to be used than if your flier arrived in the mail on the same day as fifty other such releases.

There is probably a cable TV station that broadcasts in your area. Get to know the producer because a certain amount of time is allotted to public issues such as education. Although the time given for public affairs is often not prime time, this is still another way to get your message across. You will have a better case in asking for air time if several towns within the TV station's broadcasting area have similar concerns. Therefore, you should keep in touch with other organizations that have a similar agenda.

Your organization should consider writing its own quarterly newsletter. The best of these are crisply written and focused on particular problems. State what the present condition is, why it is intolerable and why your plan for change is necessary. The ideal newsletter is an 8 × 11″ sheet of paper folded in half. That format gives you the availability to write on four pages. Anything larger probably will not be read.

Most people just will not care about your organization or your initiatives; or, stated less harshly, people will not stay informed about your beliefs and your cause unless you inform them. Accurate facts and a truthfully told story are your allies. They will help people remember your cause. Don't oversell. Your reputation is in on the line every time you communicate.

# Little Things Mean A Lot

The most important thing is to thank anyone for any support you have received. This point is obvious, yet it is often overlooked. Local change will work on trust and goodwill. You are not paying people for their work, but appreciation and a sincere 'thank you' is about as good.

Make some people in your group available for community talks. Publicize their availability to local organizations and to the general public. Go before church groups, municipal bodies, service groups such as Rotary, Lions, and Kiwanis to make your points. It will not only bring people to your cause, but blunt the arguments of the bureaucracy. Send only extremely well-informed people who are able to stay on the issue at all times. Know the arguments inside out and keep pounding the message home. If you are right on the merits of the issue and tell your story well, you will win!

Too often, the temptation is to have anyone from your organization speak at any time. This sometimes creates mistakes of great proportions, especially when your organization is young. Your first issues are litmus tests of your credibility. If you are found wanting, no matter how righteous your cause, other people will say, 'They really don't know how to get their act together.' However, if you move at a steady pace, every time you achieve a victory, the total organization rises in stature. Therefore, don't risk the embarrassment of exposing some of your well-intentioned people who know only half of the issue or people who cannot think well on their feet. In the beginning have few, but very good people to represent you at public forums.

When addressing envelopes, handwrite some and use adhesive mailing labels on others for quick mass mailings. Your organization must know to use the right technique for a particular situation. Bulk mail procedures can save money. Learn the rules and save dollars.

Select a logo so people can immediately identify with your organization. The name of your organization, of course, is important, but so is the logo. People who spend hundreds and thousands of dollars in advertising know that, before it is remembered, the name must be repeated over and over again. The logo must remind people of your name and vice versa.

# Staying Power

The most important thing that your organization must do is to keep at the total agenda. Keep track of where you are, the progress that you are making, the problems you are having and what you intend to do about solving them.

Keep documenting the inefficiencies and ineptness of the present school board and the operation for the particular schools that you are targeting. This running agenda of where you are with respect to the total agenda will serve you well.

# Do It!

It will take time, but you will overcome. You will learn and improve as you go on. And since the board of education and employees are defending a system that has serious flaws, no matter how resourceful they are, or politically smart, you will prevail. But it will take organization, hard work, and above all, staying power if you are to gain control. Poor schools and their leaders have hunkered down for years and outlasted groups of parents, continuing on their merry way of ineptitude. Frequently, this occurred because there was not a comprehensive plan for reform and parents were baffled by the sheer complexity of the schools. Puzzled and ultimately discouraged, parents retreated, leaving control of the schools in the hands of the people responsible for the problems.

In *How Schools* Really *Work* you have the beginnings of a comprehensive plan for improvement, which you can develop and augment in light of your own experience. Parents and other caring citizens can come together and take control of their schools. These approaches *will* work in your community, and your children will benefit each and every year.

# References

1. Gary Sykes, 'The Deal,' *Wilson Quarterly,* Vol. 8 (November 1, 1984).
2. Wilbur Brookover, *Schools Can Make a Difference.* East Lansing: Michigan State University, 1977.
3. Michael Rutter, *Fifteen Thousand Hours: Secondary Schools and Their Effects on Children.* Cambridge: Harvard University Press, 1979).
4. Gilbert T. Sewell, *Necessary Lessons: Decline and Renewal in American Schools* (New York: Free Press, 1983).
5. Joseph Adelson, 'Why the Schools May Not Improve,' *Commentary,* October 1984.
6. Joseph Adelson, 'How the Schools Were Ruined,' *Commentary,* July l983.
7. Marsha Levine and Roberta Tractman, *American Business and the Public School.* New York: Teachers College Press, Columbia University, l988.
8. Niccolo Machiavelli, *The Prince.* New York: Dover, l992.
9. Saul Alinsky, *Rules for Radicals.* New York: Random House, 1971.
10. Lee Staples, *Roots to Power: A Manual for Grassroots Organizing.* New York: Praeger, 1984.
11. Philip and Susan Jones, *Parents Unite.* New York: Wyden Books, 1976.
12. Robert Bailey, *Radicals in Urban Politics: The Alinsky Approach.* Chicago: University of Chicago Press, 1974.
13. Douglas P. Bilken, *Community Organizing: Theory and Practice.* Englewood Cliffs: Prentice Hall, 1983.

# Index